TEAMWORK

UNITED IN VICTORY

Jay Jennings

Silver Burdett Press

Published by Silver Burdett Press, Inc., a division of Simon & Schuster, Inc.,
Prentice Hall Bldg., Englewood Cliffs, NJ 07632.

Designer: Greg Wozney
Project Editor: Emily Easton
Manufactured in the United States of America
10 9 8 7 6 5 4 3 2 1
Library of Congress Cataloging-in-Publication Data
Jennings, Jay.
Teamwork : united in victory / by Jay Jennings.
p.   cm. — (Sports triumphs)
Summary: Profiles athletes who feel their success is due to teamwork. Includes Jackie
Joyner-Kersee and Bob Kersee, the 1969 New York Jets, and Candy Costie and Tracie
Ruiz. 1. Athletes—United States—Biography—Juvenile literature. 2. Teamwork
(Sports)—Juvenile literature. [1. Athletes. 2. Teamwork (Sports) I.
Title.   II. Series.
GV697.A1J46 1990
796'.092'2 —dc20
[B]   90-37493
ISBN 0- 382-24106-1 (lib. bdg.)   CIP
0-382-24113-4 (pbk.)   AC

Cover photo: © Steven E. Sutton from duomo

Acknowledgments

This book is not the result of one man's effort, but of much teamwork. I wish to thank the following people for their help, advice and work: Joy Duckett Cain, Paul Depta of the Cambridge (Mass.) Public Library, Roger Mooney, Craig Neff, Merrell Noden, Kenny Moore, Ed Swift, and Demmie Stathoplos.

Thanks once again go out to my editor, Emily Easton, and my agent, Kris Dahl at International Creative Management.

My wife Jessica Green was a patient reader of the manuscript and an inspiration throughout its writing. She is a perfect teammate.

Photo Acknowledgments

All Sport: Pages vi (All Sport/Tony Duffy), 5 (Allsport USA/Dave Stock), 6 (All Sport/Tony Duffy), 9 (All Sport/Tony Duffy), 12 (All Sport/Steve Powell), 19, 38 (All Sport/Dave Cannon), 41 (All Sport/Bob Martin), 45, 48 (All Sport/Tony Duffy), 51 (All Sport/Steve Powell), 52 (All Sport/Tony Duffy), 54 (All Sport/Tony Duffy).

duomo: Page 21 (duomo/Paul J. Sutton).

Focus on Sports: Pages 24, 29, 35.

NFL Photos: Page 33.

Sports Illustrated: Pages 20, 43.

FROM THE AUTHOR

Few pleasures in sport equal the thrill of watching a team execute a play flawlessly. The quarterback drops back to pass, the linemen keep the defenders away from him, and he lofts a perfect spiral downfield to the speeding receiver, who never breaks stride as the ball drops into his hands. "Just like we drew it up," coaches say afterward, referring to the chalk lines on a blackboard they have used to design the play. Such plays are good examples of cooperation and athletic ability, and you will read about many of them here.

More important, you will read about the teams that produced such plays and performances over and over again. They are the ones who understood teamwork. The major sports of hockey and football provide us with dramatic examples: the 1980 United States Olympic hockey team and the 1969 Super Bowl champion New York Jets. These teams are represented here because they are more than just a collection of athletes who made great plays. They possessed qualities beyond mere athletic ability that helped them to win.

You may be surprised by the variety of sports and people who represent the idea of teamwork. Though many trophies have only one name engraved on them, an individual like Jackie Joyner-Kersee knows that her success is earned with help. Teams of only two people, like ice dancers Jayne Torvill and Christopher Dean and synchronized swimmers Candy Costie and Tracie Ruiz, show that both similar and very different personalities can develop the characteristics of teamwork that add up to victory.

The athletes profiled here all realized that they could not have accomplished everything they did by themselves. No matter how many different forms teamwork may assume, its essence is the same: people working together to become greater than they could be alone.

Jay Jennings

CONTENTS

With Bob's coaching in the heptathlon, Jackie improved by leaps and bounds.

JACKIE JOYNER-KERSEE AND BOB KERSEE

Track's Wedded Winners

Jackie Joyner-Kersee has been called more than once "the best female athlete in the world." She has also been called, with apologies to Bo Jackson, "the best athlete in the world *period*." She has won two Olympic medals in the heptathlon, the most grueling track and field test a woman can undertake. She has also won an Olympic medal in the long jump and hopes to win more medals—possibly in different events—in 1992, when the Olympics will be held in Barcelona, Spain. Along with her sister-in-law Florence Griffith Joyner, who is married to her older brother Al, Joyner-Kersee was the star of the 1988 Seoul Olympics.

The heptathlon (the Greek root hept- means "seven") consists of seven track and field events contested over two days in the following order—100-meter hurdles, high jump, shot put, 200-meter dash, long jump, javelin, and 800-meter run. Competitors must develop strength, speed, coordination, and flexibility. Times, distances, and heights are assigned points under a complex system, and the athlete with the most points at the end of the second day wins the competition.

Though the athlete competes alone in all the events, there is an element of teamwork involved. Perhaps more than in other track and field contests, a heptathlon coach can guide an athlete through the demanding training schedule needed to maintain excellence in so many events. With too much weight training for strength, the athlete will not be flexible enough for the hurdles. Putting too much emphasis on speed might cause a lack of power and loss of distance in the shot put and javelin throw. Training must be carefully monitored and controlled. The coach must be an expert in many events and know the athlete's capabilities.

Joyner-Kersee has just such a coach in Bob Kersee. But he is more than that. He is also her husband. Their partnership is an unusual one in the world of sports, one that has benefited both of them. He has helped her reach her potential as an athlete, and she has pushed him to improve as a coach. At home, they are a team as well, splitting up household chores and doing favors for each other.

Jackie and Bob are not immune to the problems all married couples who work together face. They sometimes have disagreements both as husband and wife and as coach and athlete, but mostly they share in the joy of working and winning together. As any successful team, they inspire and push each other to excel.

He often waits with more than a coach's concern for her health when she completes a workout or race. In 1982, she developed asthma, a chronic disease that hinders breathing. She takes medication to control it, and though it hasn't given her problems in competition, Bob carefully monitors her condition and gives her the medication or water at the end of a tough race.

They met when Jackie Joyner was a freshman at the University of California at Los Angeles (UCLA) in 1980, where she had been awarded a scholarship to play basketball. Joyner excelled at other sports as well, and she also made the UCLA track team. That season, the 26-year-old Kersee became an assistant women's track coach specializing in **sprinters** and hurdlers. Though she was mainly a long jumper at the time, Kersee immediately saw the athletic potential in her 5′ 10″, 150-pound frame. Jackie had teased him about his interest in her, saying, "It was athlete at first sight."

At first their relationship was simply one between an athlete and a coach. Kersee was, like many coaches, a stern disciplinarian on the field. His father was an officer in the Navy, and there was something of military strictness and precision in his manner. Joyner-Kersee told

Life magazine: "I only knew him as this coach who was always screaming like a madman at his athletes."

Then in January of 1981, Jackie heard that her mother had been stricken with meningitis, an infection that attacks the membranes around the brain and spinal cord. Jackie's mother never recovered. She was only 38. At the funeral, Jackie was strong. Although her brother Al was older, Jackie had always been the one that everyone in her family looked to for guidance, and she didn't want to lose control of her emotions.

Her mother was the most important person in Jackie's life. Jackie learned many virtues from her mother, who worked as a nurse's assistant in East St. Louis, Illinois.

TRACK TALK

foul: stepping on or beyond the boundary allowed during the run-up or approach of a field event; the jump or throw which results is not counted.

infield: the grassy area contained within the circumference of a track; usually the site of a few field events and a warm-up area for the athletes.

pentathlon: a five-event track and field competition primarily for women, which has now been replaced by the seven-event heptathlon.

personal best: the lowest time, greatest distance, or highest point total an athlete has achieved in his or her specialty; also called a "PR" or "personal record."

sprinter: an athlete who specializes in running short races, up to or including the 400 meters.

track club: a group of athletes who train together, usually under one coach, and compete as a team against other clubs in meets.

triple jump: a field event in which an athlete completes three leaps during one attempt, first landing on the take-off foot, then on the opposite foot, and finally with both feet in the sand pit.

Mary Joyner taught her four children to be polite and hardworking. Jackie's father, Al, worked at various trades until he landed a steady railway job, which kept him away from home much of the time. Mary held the family together and shielded them from the bad influences and danger of their rough East St. Louis neighborhood.

Located across the Mississippi River from St. Louis, Missouri, East St. Louis is an impoverished area that is mainly black. Abandoned houses and boarded-up factories are everywhere. In the ten years before Jackie left for UCLA, the population of the city dropped from 70,169 to 55,200 as people fled from its problems. Crime and drug use are widespread.

When the Joyner children were growing up, temptations lurked all around them. Their parents, who had married when they were teenagers, tried to teach them values that would allow them to survive and succeed. Schoolwork was important. Low grades brought groundings. Fearful that an early marriage or pregnancy might restrict Jackie's life and keep her in the ghetto, her mother didn't allow Jackie to date until she was eighteen.

The Joyners were poor, but the love and strength in the family carried them through. Jackie told *The New York Times Magazine*: "We didn't know we were poor. We didn't have a lot, but we knew our mother and father were doing their very best." Sometimes the pipes froze in the winter and they had to heat water on the stove. Sometimes they had so little to eat that they made meals out of bread and mayonnaise.

Jackie spent much of her youth at the Mary E. Brown Community Center, where she read, took dance classes, learned cheerleading and began to participate in sports. During her first three years of elementary school, she was placed in an enrichment program and remained an excellent student all the way through Lincoln High School, where she graduated in the top 10 percent of her class.

She accomplished even greater feats outside the classroom in athletics. Her high school track coach, Nino Fennoy, who first met her during a summer camp when she was nine, had sent a number of Lincoln athletes out of the ghetto on track scholarships, and he nurtured her raw talent. At age nine, after one meet, she came home as the winner of five first-place awards. That accomplishment convinced her brother Al to take up track as well.

Jackie was so versatile that she began competing in the five-event **pentathlon** (100-meter hurdles, shot put, high jump, long jump, and 800-meter run) and eventually won a national junior championship. Jackie also excelled on Lincoln's basketball, volleyball, and track teams. By the time she finished school, she held the state record in the long jump at 20' 7½" and had been offered a basketball scholarship to UCLA.

She took the long trip West and stayed over Christmas that first year, assuring her mother over the phone that she would be back home for spring break. Tragically, her mother died the next month.

When Jackie returned from the funeral, she found a sympathetic ear in the assistant track coach, Bob Kersee. The coach had heard about the tragedy, and he told her that his mother had also died at a young age. She gradually found that she could talk to him about anything and that the coach whom she only knew as a loud voice barking orders at athletes had a sensitive side.

He was helping her on the field as well. Though the long jump was her specialty and she planned to concentrate on the event in college, he thought the power and speed of her legs might serve her well in other events, too. He suggested she try the heptathlon. (After 1980, the major women's multievent competition became the heptathlon when the javelin and 200-meter dash were added to the pentathlon.) She took his advice, while continuing to compete in the long jump as a separate event.

She won the National Collegiate Athletic Association (NCAA) heptathlon championship in her sophomore and junior years and was also an all-conference basketball forward. During 1983–84, she took a year off from basketball in order to concentrate on track and prepare for the 1984 Olympics in Los Angeles.

Two weeks before the Games, she injured her hamstring, which is any of the three muscles located at the back of the thigh. It is very difficult to run or jump with such an injury, but she was determined not to miss the Olympics. Her brother Al had also qualified for the Games in the **triple jump**, an event accurately described by its former name, the "hop, step, and jump."

Competition in Los Angeles was not as intense as in past Olympics because the Soviet Union and some of the countries in Eastern Europe chose not to attend. They boycotted the Los Angeles Games in retaliation for the American boycott of the Moscow Games in 1980. 1984 was the first year the heptathlon was made an Olympic event. Since the best heptathletes were from Eastern Europe, Joyner-Kersee was expected to win the gold medal.

Through four events, Joyner-Kersee was leading comfortably. Next came the long jump, her favorite and best event. The hamstring was bothering her, and her first two jumps were not counted because of **fouls**, which resulted when she left the ground beyond the allowed line. She had to be very careful on her third and last jump; if she fouled again, she would get no points for that event.

She was too careful and only jumped 20′ ½″, six inches shorter than she had cleared even in high school. That allowed Australia's Glynis Nunn to get within striking distance with only two events—the javelin and the 800-meter run—remaining. Nunn stayed close after the javelin, and the 800 meters was Jackie's worst event.

Meanwhile, Al had taken the lead in the triple jump with a leap of 56′ 7½″. As the

800 meters started, he cheered Jackie on from the **infield** grass, even running beside her along the final turn. She could afford to finish no more than a couple of seconds behind Nunn to keep her lead and win the gold. As they came down the straightaway during the final lap, Jackie tried to stay as close as she could but was laboring with her injury.

She crossed the finish line three-tenths of a second too slow and lost the gold medal to Nunn by only five points, 6,390 to 6,385. The Joyner family, however, did go home with one gold medal; Al's jump was good enough to win. Later, when Al found Jackie crying, he tried to comfort her. She told him that she wasn't crying because she had lost, but because she was so happy he had won.

The Olympics were a big success for Bob Kersee. The seven athletes he coached—including Jackie and Al—won ten medals, more than many countries. He was, however, convinced that Jackie could do better. He knew in his heart that she could break the 7,000-point mark in the heptathlon, something no woman had ever done, and he wanted to help her achieve that milestone.

As they trained and talked through the following months, the two became closer friends. Though Bob was eight years older, the age difference didn't seem as wide any more. Both of them had matured. Bob had become head coach of the UCLA women's track team. Jackie had graduated with a degree in history and communications and was out on her own, free from the pressures of being a student. She began to train and compete as a member of the World Class Athletic Club, the **track club** Bob coached in addition to his duties at UCLA.

Jackie and Bob began spending more of their free time together, going out to dinner or for drives along the coast. Jackie described the development of their relationship to *Life* magazine: "One night he

Bob and Jackie's friendship as coach and athlete eventually grew into love.

came by and said, 'Let's go to the beach.' Nothing happened, but you know how you can just feel something? From that point on, I just knew."

He proposed to her during a Houston Astros baseball game, and they were married in January of 1986.

Six months later, the newlyweds arrived in Moscow for the Goodwill Games, an international athletic competition similar to the Olympics. She was primed for the competition. In the first event, the 100-meter hurdles, she ran the distance in a blistering 12.85 seconds for a new **personal best**. She completed the first day with a 6′ 2″ high jump, a 48′ 5¼″ shot put, and a

The heptathlon required Joyner-Kersee to develop strength for the shot put.

23-seconds-flat 200 meters.

She was on a pace to break the world record of 6,946 points and possibly reach the 7,000-point goal. On the second day, Jackie sailed 23 feet through the air on her first long jump attempt. The distance was a new heptathlon record and just nine inches short of her American record in that individual event. Bob was excited, nervous, and amazed by his wife's performance. He had set high goals for her, but he hardly expected anything like this.

On her first throw, the javelin flew 163' 7", another personal best. With only the 800 meters remaining, she had accumulated an astonishing total of 6,184 points. She breezed around the track twice in 2 minutes, 10.02 seconds for a final total of 7,148 points. She had bettered the old world record by more than 200 points!

Just a month later she broke that record at a meet in Houston, Texas, when the temperature reached 100 degrees. She told the press afterward, "I had my doubts I would make it coming around the quarter in the 800, but all the time I was running, I kept remembering what Bobby says in the morning when I'm doing my roadwork. He says, 'Go to your arms. Start pumping.' As soon as I did, then I started to relax."

During their first year of marriage, Jackie's record-breaking drew attention and honors, even though the heptathlon was not generally well-known or well-covered by the media. She won the 1986 Broderick Cup as the top collegiate woman athlete of the year, was named by *Track & Field News* as their Woman Athlete of 1986, and won the Sullivan Award as America's top amateur athlete, man or woman.

Bob and Jackie's closeness as husband and wife probably helps them communicate better as coach and athlete, but they try to keep the two lives separate. He shows her no favoritism in training, devoting as much time to the other athletes in his World Class Athletic Club. He has a reputation as a hard coach to please, and he points out her

mistakes and makes demands of her as he would of his other athletes. She also has strong ideas about the way she performs and trains, and while she will listen closely to Bob, she sometimes dismisses his advice and does what she feels is right.

For example, he didn't want her to compete in the Pan American Games in Indianapolis, Indiana, in 1987 because he was afraid she might be too tired to do well at the World Championships in Rome, Italy, a couple of weeks later. She followed her own heart, and at the Pan Am Games she tied the world record in the long jump. Bob, even though he objected to her presence there, was so happy for her, he was moved to tears. And later, in Rome, she won gold medals in the heptathlon and the long jump, proving that Bob's fears were unfounded.

Both are perfectionists. Kersee is a keen student, staying abreast of all the latest training developments and scientific research. He knows all about weight training, diet, muscles, massage, and techniques for throwing, running, and jumping. He sees himself as a "detail" person. He carefully studies videotapes of his athletes' performances and watches for the smallest change in form or the tiniest adjustment. What he notices may add only an inch to a long jump or shave just hundredths of a second off a sprint, but at the highest levels of track and field, those differences can decide who wins and who finishes last. Florence Griffith Joyner, who was also once coached by Kersee, told Dick Patrick, the track and field writer for *USA Today*: "One demonstration from Bobby is worth a thousand words."

Joyner-Kersee is particularly attuned to Kersee's demonstrations. Because she is so aware of every movement her body makes, she can quickly correct faults spotted by him. If he occasionally yells at her (as he does with all his athletes), she knows she needs it and appreciates that he is only trying to help her improve.

At home, they lead a very quiet, normal

life. After a day of training, while Jackie is at a physical therapist's having her leg muscles massaged, Bob will cook a dinner of vegetables, pasta, or chicken. And when Bob himself wants a massage, Jackie obliges. Both of them say that they are "best friends" as well as husband and wife.

After the successes at the Pan Am Games and in Rome, it was time to prepare for the 1988 Olympics in Seoul, South Korea. Joyner-Kersee had waited four long years for another shot at the Olympic gold that had escaped her in Los Angeles. The first step to Seoul was the U.S. Trials, held in Indianapolis.

For Joyner-Kersee, the Trials were almost a formality. She was already the only woman ever to score 7,000 points or more in the heptathlon, and she was one of the best long jumpers in the world. The Trials were to be a kind of family outing: Bob would be there with Jackie, and her brother Al would be competing in the triple jump. His wife, Florence Griffith Joyner, was running in the 100- and 200- meter dashes.

"Flo-Jo" dazzled everyone with her speed, setting a world record in the 100 and a U.S. record in the 200, and her style, wearing a lacy, full-length bodysuit. Joyner-Kersee was more quietly clothed but just as stunning in her performances.

As in the 1984 Olympics, Al was competing in the triple jump while his sister was running the 800 meters during the heptathlon. This time, he was the one who needed cheering on. He had already jumped twice and was down to his final try. As the cheers rose for Jackie on her final lap, Al made his run, took his hop-step, skipped, and leaped, landing in the sand 57' 7½" from the takeoff board. Jackie's finishing time in the 800 put her beyond her old world record. Al's distance was only good enough for fourth place. The 1984 triple jump gold medalist didn't make the 1988 team. When Jackie heard the news, she cried for her brother and promised to dedicate her performance in Seoul to him.

Before the Olympics Bob worried that Jackie had done almost too well in Indianapolis and that she couldn't top that performance. On the first day of the heptathlon competition in Seoul, Bob nervously followed Jackie through the first four events. In the 100-meter hurdles, she set a personal best by running a time of 12.69 seconds. That was better than her

THE HEPTATHLON

First Day events

100-meter Hurdles: The heptathletes begin competition by racing 100 meters, while stepping over ten barriers, or hurdles, which are 36 inches high. There is no penalty for knocking over the hurdles.

High Jump: In this event, the competitors try to clear a crossbar balanced on two supporting poles. The crossbar is raised with each clearance, and a jumper is allowed three tries at each height.

Shot Put: The athletes heave an eight pound, 13 ounce metal ball, called a "shot," by holding it at shoulder level and pushing it away from the body. The contestant must remain within a throwing circle which is seven feet in diameter.

200-meter Dash: This sprint covers one-half of a 400-meter oval track and is run around the track's second curve.

Second Day Events

Long Jump: The second day begins with the heptathletes leaping for distance from a running start. The jump is measured from the front of the take-off board (the athletes are not allowed to leave the ground beyond this board) to the closest mark the jumper makes in a sandy landing area.

Javelin Throw: From a running start, the athlete throws a pointed spear called a "javelin" for distance. The javelin must land point first.

800-meter Run: The competition ends with this test of stamina in which the heptathletes run two laps around the 400-meter track.

Bob and Jackie took a victory lap together after her gold medal win in Seoul.

world-record time in the Trials.

During the high jump, however, she strained her knee and only jumped 6′ 1¼″, nearly three inches below her best height.

With the knee taped, she heaved the shot 51′ 10″, good enough for second in the event among the heptathletes. Finishing the day

with the 200 meters, she ran the distance in 22.56 seconds. Her first-day total of 4,264 led the other heptathletes but was far behind a world-record pace.

The knee was bothering her the next day. The long jump was first, but her takeoff leg was the opposite of the hurt one, so it didn't hamper her performance. She soared with a leap of 23′ 10¼″—the best ever in the heptathlon.

Before the javelin, Bob and Jackie had one of their coach-athlete disagreements. Bob thought she needed to have the knee taped before her throw, but Jackie thought it would limit her flexibility. Bob won the argument, but not without a compromise. "This girl is so stubborn," he said, "we had to give her scissors to cut the tape off if she didn't like it." She left it on and threw the javelin 149′ 10″, which she later described as "disgusting."

She already had such a substantial lead that she knew the gold medal was hers, but with only 776 points gained in the javelin, she didn't know if she could set a new world record. She had long ago so outdistanced her opposing heptathletes that she became disappointed if she didn't set a world record every time she competed. As Bob told *USA Today* track writer Dick Patrick: "Jackie's got to think of the world record as another competitor. I've named it the Wilhemina World Record."

The stadium had nearly emptied after the men's 100-meter dash, which featured Ben Johnson and Carl Lewis. Those who left missed seeing Joyner-Kersee beat Wilhemina, finishing the 800 meters in a time of 2 minutes, 8.51 seconds for a total of 7,291 points. She had her gold medal and her world record.

When she crossed the finish line, Bob was right there as always to hug her. They waved to the remaining fans together— coach and athlete, husband and wife.

JACKIE JOYNER-KERSEE

1984 OLYMPIC PERFORMANCE

Heptathlon
Silver Medal

Event	Distance / Time	Points
100-Meter Hurdles	13.63 seconds	914
High Jump	5 feet 10¾ inches	1,031
Shot Put	47 feet 2½ inches	861
200-Meter Dash	24.05 seconds	933
Long Jump	20 feet ½ inch	930
Javelin	146 feet 1 inch	835
800-Meter Run	2 minutes 13.03 seconds	881
Total		6,385

1988 OLYMPIC PERFORMANCE

Heptathlon
Gold Medal

Event	Distance / Time	Points
100-Meter Hurdles	12.69 seconds	1,172
High Jump	6 feet 1¼ inches	1,054
Shot Put	51 feet 10 inches	915
200-Meter Dash	22.56 seconds	1,123
Long Jump	23 feet 10¼ inches	1,264
Javelin	149 feet 10 inches	776
800-Meter Run	2 minutes 8.51 seconds	987
Total		7,291

Long Jump
Gold Medal

24 feet 3½ inches (new Olympic record)

Until the 1980 Olympics, the U.S. players were just talented individuals.

THE 1980 UNITED STATES OLYMPIC HOCKEY TEAM

Miracle Boys

The year 1980 was a troubled one for the United States. Prices of U.S. products were soaring. Militants in Iran held Americans hostage at the U.S. embassy in Tehran. President Jimmy Carter condemned the Soviet invasion of Afghanistan, and at his suggestion the U.S. Olympic Committee was considering a boycott of the 1980 Summer Olympics in Moscow.

Since then the Soviet army has left Afghanistan and relations between the two countries have improved. But in 1980, the Winter Olympics were held in February in Lake Placid, New York, against this backdrop of international tension and turmoil. No one expected the American athletes to do very well. Only speed skater Eric Heiden and a handful of others looked like strong contenders for gold medals. Then, almost out of nowhere, the 1980 U.S. Olympic hockey team emerged as a source of pride for Americans. With youthful enthusiasm as one of their few assets, twenty Americans banded together to accomplish what few thought possible. In the two weeks of the Olympics they proved to America and the world that a team can become more than its individual parts.

But first they had to *become* a team....

In 1979, when Herb Brooks, the hockey coach at the University of Minnesota, was asked to choose the U.S. team and prepare it for the 1980 Olympics, he faced several problems. In a college program, players spend years learning the coach's system, learning about each other, learning to play together.

Forming the Olympic team was different. In only a few months, Brooks had to take a group of diverse players and mold them quickly into a unit that could compete with the best hockey teams in the world. Most of the American players starred for their college teams. Most of them had been drafted by the National Hockey League (NHL) and would try to make hockey a career. They were headstrong, confident, ambitious young men.

To the players, the opportunity to play in the Olympics was a stepping-stone on the way to the professional ranks. By performing well in Lake Placid, they might be able to squeeze a few more dollars out of the professional teams when they signed contracts. They could hardly hope for more out of the Olympics. Certainly they couldn't hope for a gold medal.

After all, Olympic hockey was dominated by the team from the Soviet Union. They had won gold medals at every winter Olympics since 1964.

The Soviets were the opposite of the U.S. team. Unlike the U.S. players, many of whom had never been on the same rink before, the Soviets had played together for years and knew each other as well as teammates could. When hockey writers and fans described them, they frequently called the team a "machine."

The Soviet Union has a very advanced system for identifying and training athletes. If a hockey player shows very early in his life—before he is a teenager, for example—that he has superior skills, the government will support his training and bring him together with other young stars. By the time Soviet players are in their 20s and 30s,

they have played with all the country's best players for years.

When the Soviets visited the United States in 1979 to play the NHL All-Stars, many expected North America's professional players to end the Soviet dominance of hockey. The NHL had the best players in the world, people said. If only they were allowed to play in the Olympics, they would show the Soviets a thing or two. Surprisingly, the Soviets dominated the Challenge Cup, as the matchup was called, and wiped away any doubt that the Soviet team was the best in the world.

The task Brooks had in front of him seemed impossible. He had seven months to choose and train a team to beat the Soviets. How?

He began with a test, but not a physical test. He already knew that the 68 players who had been invited to Colorado Springs, Colorado, to try out for the team had the skills to play the game. They were college stars, All-Americas. The test he gave them was a written examination of over 300 questions. Some of the players objected to the exam. They were there to play hockey, not to take tests. That was for college.

Brooks was looking for a special kind of player, one who could adapt to Brooks's style of play. He didn't care if the best individual players didn't make the team. Brooks told *Sports Illustrated* magazine: "The ignorant people, the self-centered people, the people who don't want to expand their thoughts, they're not going to be the real good athletes." He was looking for open-mindedness, because he was going to break down everything they knew about hockey and remold them into a team.

Before long he had whittled down his choices to twenty-six players who would train for the Olympic team. Sixteen players were from Minnesota, six from Massachusetts, and two each from Michigan and Wisconsin.

The new style of play he introduced he

called "sophisticated pond hockey," which combined the rough defensive **bodychecking** of American hockey with the skill and free-skating of the European game. The size of the rink in international play was part of the reason for this change. In North America, the rinks for college and professional games are 85 feet wide. In international play, the rink is 100 feet wide. This extra space would allow the offensive players—the forwards—to move around more, to cross and **feint** and weave, to rush to open ice rather than skate in a straight line to the goal.

The Soviets themselves played in this style. How could a team play the Soviet type of game with less talented players and still win? That was the dilemma Brooks faced.

He knew his players were not as talented as the Soviets. There was nothing he could do about that. He worked on areas he could control, areas where the U.S. could equal the Soviets. He started with stamina. The Soviets were in better shape than any other team in the world. To help his team reach that level of fitness, he consulted experts from other sports where Americans had kept up with the Soviets, swimming and track, for example.

Then he applied their ideas to his team. He made his players run, skate without the puck, and do "line drills," or "Herbies," as the players called them in tribute to their coach. A player would start at the goal line, sprint to the **blue line** and back, then sprint to the **red line** and back, then to the far blue line and back, finally to the opposite goal line and back. Brooks drove the players through sets and sets of Herbies until they were exhausted.

Brooks was hard on his players. He wasn't the kind of coach whom the players considered a friend. He kept his distance from them. He knew that if the players became too close to him, they might not take him as seriously when he wanted them to work harder. He gave no one a break, not

even his favorite players. If the Americans were to beat the Soviets, or if they were even to earn the chance to play them, they would need to have someone motivating them the whole time. He couldn't point to the Olympics to inspire them. It was half a year away. He had to create an adversary for them to become united against long before then. Herb Brooks, by his own plan, was that adversary.

PUCK TALK

blue lines: measured 60 feet towards the center of the rink from each goal line; they mark each team's defensive zone and are mainly used to determine offside, a penalty when an offensive player enters the zone before the puck.

body check: using the upper body to block an opponent from the side or front.

deflection: a pass or shot that bounces off a skate, a player, or a stick.

draft: the system used by the National Hockey League to select amateur players from colleges, high schools, and club teams; the league's teams take turns choosing and so acquire the sole rights within the league to have that player play for their team.

exhibition: a game which doesn't count in the official standings, but is played merely for practice or charity.

feint: faking a shot or move in order to draw an opponent out of position.

forecheck: closely guarding an opponent in his own zone while attempting to take the puck from him.

forward: any of the three attacking offensive positions: center, left wing, or right wing.

power play: the offensive push of a team which has an advantage in numbers because one or more opposing players are off the ice serving penalties.

red line: the line which divides the rink in half.

slap shot: an attempt to score a goal by raising the stick off the ice and striking the puck from behind.

Brooks perhaps knew better than anyone else what the opportunity to play in the Olympics meant to an athlete. In 1960, he had been the final player cut from the U.S. Olympic hockey team, the last team to defeat the Soviets for the gold medal. If his players got that same chance, he wanted them to be ready.

A coach can only do so much, though. The players are the ones on the ice.

In a competition like the Olympics, when all the months of work can come down to one game, it is important to have a strong, consistent goaltender. In 1960, Jack McCartan was in the American net and keyed the U.S. to its lone hockey gold medal. The goalie is often the one who determines the character of the team. He is the line of last defense.

Jim Craig was the U.S.A.'s goaltender in 1980. He played for Boston University, which won the national collegiate championship while he was there. In the three years when he was in their net, the Terriers won 55 games, lost only 3 and tied 1. The Atlanta Flames of the NHL had **drafted** him, but he postponed turning professional in order to try out for the Olympic team. It was a tough decision for him because his family could have used the money a professional career would bring him. His widower father was out of work, and Craig had two little brothers still at home. But he made the sacrifice, becoming a steadying influence on the team, coolly swatting away shots during the team's 61-game **exhibition** schedule.

He was one of the most accepting of Brooks' training regimen. About a month before the Olympics, Craig said, "It's the most demanding training I have ever seen, or heard of. It's hard work, no time off, and no chance to relax. But we needed it....It's been worth the pain."

The captain of the team, Mike Eruzione, was also from Boston University, though he was a couple of years older than Craig. When he wasn't offered a contract from any NHL team, he played as an amateur in hockey's minor leagues. His family tried to persuade him to give up the sport and try another occupation, but he continued to play for pure love of the game. He hustled all the time and was a fiery competitor on the ice. The word *eruzione* in Italian means "explosion." "I know I'm not that good a hockey player," he told Phil Hersh of *The Sporting News*. "I know I can't skate and I fall down a lot. But there are such things as intangibles, and I think I possess a lot of them."

Perhaps the best player on the team was **forward** Mark Johnson, a smooth skater and quiet talker who led by example. He always deflected praise away from himself to his teammates. His father was the coach at the University of Wisconsin, and he had been taught the basics of the game since his youth.

One of the players selected for the team was a constant reminder of the 1960 triumph over the Soviets. Dave Christian's father and uncle had played for that gold medal team. It is impossible to measure the effect of such a legacy on the U.S. squad, but successful teams are always composed of such emotional factors.

The last game of the grueling exhibition schedule was against the Soviet Olympic team in a game at Madison Square Garden in New York City. Three days later the U.S. would meet Sweden in their opening Olympic game. The tour up to that point had been successful. Against various college, NHL, and foreign teams, the Americans had posted a record of 42 wins, 15 losses, and 1 tie. Craig said before the game: "They could blow us out and it might hurt us, or maybe we would take the game as a kind of exhibition and not let it mean that much. We are so young that it's hard to tell how we all feel."

They undoubtedly felt worse when the Soviets confidently skated out onto the ice and manhandled the young team by a score of 10–3.

The United States went into the Olympic tournament ranked seventh best of the twelve teams. The tournament was organized into two divisions of six teams each. After a first round of games, the two teams with the best won-lost records in each division would move to the "medal" round. Those four teams would play a round-robin schedule (every team plays every other team once), which would determine the winners of the gold, silver, and bronze medals.

The U.S. found itself with two tough opening games against Sweden and Czechoslovakia. The Swedes were as skilled as any team in the world but sometimes didn't play up to their ability. If the Americans stayed close, they would have a good chance to win. Since the game against the Czechs would be the tougher of the two, the U.S. felt it had to either win or tie against Sweden to advance to the medal round.

When the game began, the 8,000-odd seats in the Olympic Ice Arena were only half-full. That lack of interest seemed justified when the Swedes took a 1–0 lead after the first period. In the first four minutes of the game, the U.S. had two breakaways to Sweden's goal and missed both shots. The Swedes kept Craig busy with 16 shots on goal to only 7 for the U.S.

Craig kept knocking away shots through the second period, shutting Sweden out. The U.S. players gained confidence. With only 28 seconds to go before the second intermission, right wing Dave Silk took a pass from Johnson and beat the Swedish goalie to even the score at 1–1.

In the third period, the Swedes went up 2–1 on a goal with a little more than fifteen minutes to play. Sweden guarded that lead well, and the Americans couldn't break through. With a minute to go, Brooks, in a desperation move, pulled Craig out and left the American net open while six Americans crowded into the Swedish end. Behind the Swedish net, both teams fought furiously

for the puck. It squirted out along the left boards, where Mark Pavelich scooped it away from a Swedish defenseman. He centered it perfectly to Bill Baker whose **slap shot** passed under the Swedish goalie with 27 seconds remaining.

The final score was only a tie, but the benefit to the Americans was greater than anything that would appear in the standings; they had gained a sense that they could come from behind at any time, even as the clock ticked off the final few seconds of a game.

To give themselves a chance to advance to the medal round, the Americans would have to beat the Czech team, a tougher opponent than the Swedish team. The Czechs, who had finished no worse than third in the last ten world championships, were big and strong, very similar to the Soviets, though slower than the Swedes.

When the Czechs scored with only 2:23 gone in the first period, the U.S. was forced to play catch-up again. They matched strength with strength. The American line of Buzz Schneider, Mark Pavelich, and John Harrington led the way as the Americans evened the score at 2–2 after the first period.

That trio called themselves the Iron Rangers because all of them were raised in the iron-producing Mesabi Range of northern Minnesota. The name fit. They **forechecked** the powerful Czech defensemen but were quick enough to get back to their own end so the Czechs couldn't skate away for a 3-on-2 or 2-on-1 advantage. By the end of the game, the Czechs were frustrated, the Americans were dominating, and the score was 7–3, a rout for the Americans.

Their confidence grew, as did fan interest. The arena was packed for their other games, and the young U.S. team made those fans uneasy by falling behind early, as they had in their first two games.

After giving up a quick goal, the U.S. came back to beat Norway 5–1. Against

Romania, the Americans posted an expected victory by the score of 7–2. In the last of the first-round games, the U.S. fell behind 2–0 to West Germany before winning 4–2.

The U.S.A.'s record of 4 wins, no losses, and 1 tie was good enough to put the team in the medal round with Sweden, Finland, and the U.S.S.R. Games played in the first round against other teams in the medal round counted in determining the medal winners, so the U.S.A.'s tie with Sweden was carried over, as was the U.S.S.R.'s 4–2 victory over Finland.

Such final-round eccentricities faded into the background for the U.S.A.'s next game against the Soviet Union. The Americans were finally where they wanted to be. A month before, Craig had said, "We are not awed by them. We're too young. We're so young that we kind of relish the thought of getting a shot at them."

Throughout the seven months of training and exhibitions, Brooks had subtly prepared his team for this one game. He had picked players so young and so inexperienced in international play that they didn't *know* they couldn't beat the Soviets. He had also commented on the Soviet players in a way that made it impossible for his team to take them seriously. For seven months he had said that the Soviet captain, Boris Mikhailov, looked like Stan Laurel, the thin, droopy-faced comedian of Laurel and Hardy fame. When the players looked out on the ice, they didn't see a Russian powerhouse, they saw Stan Laurel and friends.

At other times, when he felt the team needed to hear it, he would voice the opinion that the Soviets were unbeatable, that the best the Americans could hope for would be the bronze medal. But just before the game, he inspired his team with other words. "It's *meant* to be," he told them. "This is your moment and it's going to happen."

They skated out onto the ice in Lake Placid believing that. And when the Soviets took a 1–0 lead halfway through the first period, the Americans weren't worried. Why shouldn't the Soviets do what every other team had done to them? They were used to playing from behind.

Schneider, the only holdover from the 1976 Olympic team, evened the score with a 50-foot shot from the left boards. The Soviets went ahead again when Sergei Makarov scored with 2:26 to go in the period.

It looked as though that 2–1 lead would hold through the first period, but with five seconds left, Dave Christian took a desperation slap shot from beyond center ice which Soviet goalie Vladislav Tretiak blocked in front of him. As the two Soviet defensemen approached the puck from either side, Mark Johnson split between them in a flash. Four seconds remained. He picked up the puck to the left of the net as the Soviet defensemen flailed with their sticks. Three seconds. He feinted a shot and Tretiak dropped to his knees. Two seconds. Sliding farther left, Johnson flipped a shot behind the lunging goalie. Score! With one second on the clock! Instead of fighting from behind in the second period, the U.S. went into the locker room even. They had been behind so many times after the first period that starting the second period with a tie score was like a gift.

Tretiak was no longer the goalie when the teams came out for the second period. In the net was Vladimir Myshkin, who had held the NHL All-Stars scoreless in a 1979 exhibition game. He did the same to the young Americans. The Soviets got one goal and played all period in the American end, outshooting the U.S.A. 12–2. Considering the pressure he was enduring, Craig was playing brilliantly, stopping the Soviet bullets with his lightning-quick reflexes.

By the start of the third period, the crowd at the Olympic Ice Center was beginning to sense that the Russians could be beaten. Some 8,500 people began chanting "U! S! A!" at a deafening volume. The chants turned to wild, random cheering

Goalie Jim Craig stopped Soviet shots with his lightning-quick reflexes.

when, during a **power play** with 8:39 gone in the period, Johnson caught a **deflection** off a Soviet defenseman's skate and pushed the puck under Myshkin to tie the score. The Soviets appeared in shock.

Less than a minute and a half later, Eruzione picked up a puck that had bounded off the boards, waited a beat and wristed a shot under Myshkin, who was screened by his own defenseman. The U.S.A. led 4–3! The whole American team surrounded Eruzione in glee. They were ahead of the Soviets!

There were exactly ten minutes to go, but the Soviets looked as though they had already lost the game. There was desperation in the way they chased down the puck. They shot wildly, but they only

Steve Christoff's second-period goal tied the game with Finland at 1-1.

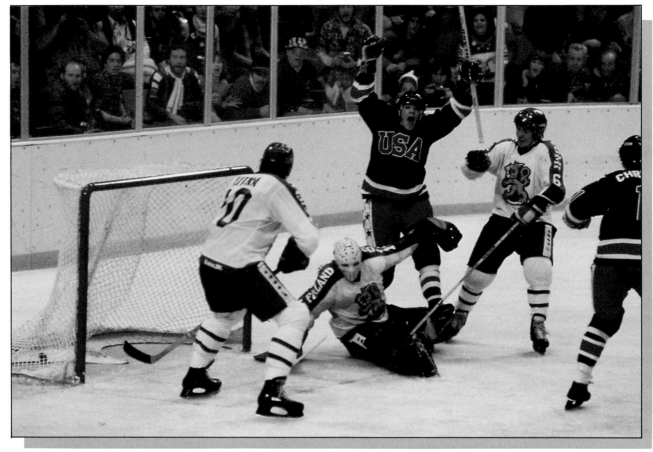

managed 9 shots on goal in the third period, compared to 18 in the first and 12 in the second. With a minute left, the Americans played keep-away with the puck in their own end. Soviet checking was hard and frantic, but they couldn't seem to control the puck. Anticipation—and noise from the crowd—grew with every tick of the clock.

Finally, when the last second elapsed, an explosion of cheers erupted from the stands. Over the noise, Americans watching on television heard announcer Al Michaels cry, "Do you believe in miracles?! Yes!" American players danced off the bench to join their teammates on the ice. It was joyous pandemonium. Players hugged and fell down and threw their sticks into the air. In the stands American flags of all sizes swayed back and forth.

Meanwhile the Soviets stood stunned at center ice, their hands resting on top of their sticks. Some of them even became caught up in the excitement of it all and smiled vaguely.

The Americans reluctantly left the ice and returned to the locker room. Once there, they were quiet, letting the monumental nature of their upset sink in. Then one of them started softly singing "God Bless America." The rest joined, though no one remembered all the words.

All across the country, spontaneous applause and cheers broke out as Americans heard the news. "We beat the Russians!" People stopped on the side of the highway and honked their horns or got out of their cars and danced. We beat the Russians! People in restaurants stopped eating and sang "The Star-Spangled Banner."

Where was Herb Brooks at the greatest

moment of his career? He had locked himself in the men's room because he thought his presence might spoil the team's happy mood. He knew they had a game remaining before they could really start celebrating. He told *Sports Illustrated*: "Finally I snuck out into the hall, and the state troopers were all standing there crying."

Everyone but Brooks seemed to have forgotten that the Olympic tournament wasn't over yet. The U.S. still had to play Finland two days later. That game would decide the final standings. If the U.S. lost, there would be no medal. According to the organization of the tournament, a win over Finland would give the Americans the gold medal, but a loss would put them fourth. The victory over the Soviets, while sweet, would feel hollow. The Americans had to finish the job.

Once again, the Finns scored first to lead the Americans, who trailed 1–0 for the sixth time in seven games. The two teams traded goals in the second period, and the Americans found themselves down again going into the third. By now, third period rallies were old hat.

Only two and a half minutes into the period, Phil Verchota tied the game at 2–2. Just over 6 minutes had passed when Rob McClanahan beat the Finnish goalie for the lead. A series of penalties gave the Finns a one-man advantage, but the Americans, in their typical way of overcoming adversity, scored a goal of their own to put the game safely out of reach, 4–2. Again the seconds ticked down on an improbable American victory.

When the game ended, Eruzione chased down the puck and scooped it up in his glove. He joined the rest of the team clustered together in celebration. One player was missing. Goalie Jim Craig skated away from the team to the side of the rink and searched the stands for his father. Someone then draped an American flag over his shoulders.

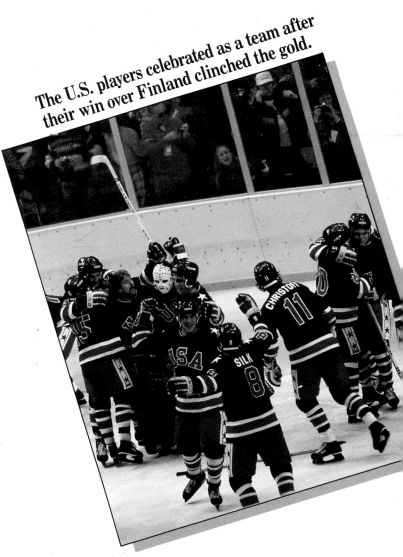

The U.S. players celebrated as a team after their win over Finland clinched the gold.

Later, at the medal ceremony in the arena, Eruzione, as captain of the team, stood on the highest level of the platform and sang the national anthem. Afterward, he exuberantly motioned for his teammates to join him. They ran to the platform and crowded onto it, celebrating as they had trained and worked and played for the last seven months—as a team.

FOR THE EXTRA POINT

Eskenazi, Gerald, et al. *Miracle on Ice*. New York: Bantam, 1980. (Advanced readers.)
Aaseng, Nathan. *Hockey: You Are the Coach*. Minneapolis: Lerner, 1983.

1980 UNITED STATES
OLYMPIC HOCKEY TEAM

USA PRELIMINARY ROUND SCORES

USA 2, Sweden 2   USA 7, Romania 2
USA 7, Czechoslovakia 3   USA 4, West Germany 2
USA 5, Norway 1

USA MEDAL-ROUND GAMES

February 22

Team				Period 1	2	3	Final
USA				2	0	2 —	4
USSR				2	1	0 —	3

	Goal	Team	Player	Assist(s)	Time
FIRST PERIOD:	1.	USSR	Krutov	Kasatonov	9:12
	2.	USA	Schneider	Pavelich	14:03
	3.	USSR	Makarov	A.Golikov	17:34
	4.	USA	Johnson	Christian, Silk	19:59
SECOND PERIOD:	5.	USSR	Maltsev	Krutov	2:18
THIRD PERIOD:	6.	USA	Johnson	Silk	8:39
	7.	USA	Eruzione	Pavelich, Harrington	10:00

SHOTS ON GOAL:

Team	Period 1	2	3	Total
USA on Tretiak, Myshkin	8	2	6	16
USSR on Craig	18	12	9	39

USA MEDAL-ROUND GAMES

February 24

Team			Period			
			1	2	3	Final
USA			0	1	3 –	4
Finland			1	1	0 –	2

	Goal	Team	Player	Assist(s)	Time
FIRST PERIOD:	1.	Finland	Povari	Leinonen	9:20
SECOND PERIOD:	2.	USA	Christoff	(Unassisted)	4:39
	3.	Finland	Leinonen	Haapalainen, Kiimalainen	6:30
THIRD PERIOD:	4.	USA	Verchota	Christian	2:25
	5.	USA	McClanahan	Johnson, Christian	6:05
	6.	USA	Johnson	Christoff	16:25

SHOTS ON GOAL:

Team	Period			
	1	2	3	Total
USA on Valtonen	14	8	7	29
Finland on Craig	7	6	10	23

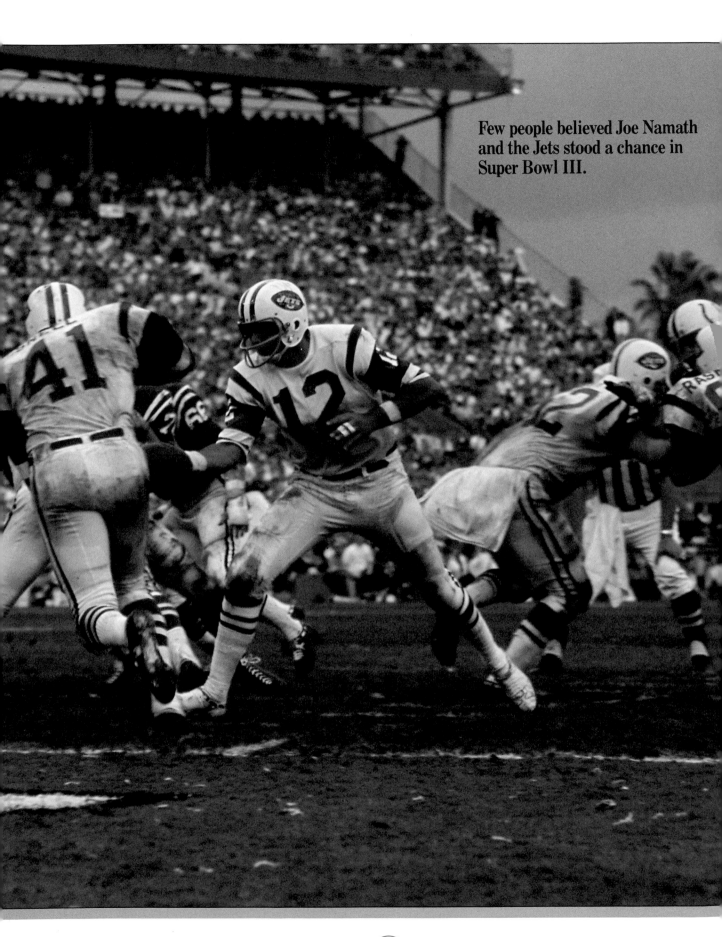

Few people believed Joe Namath and the Jets stood a chance in Super Bowl III.

THE 1968-69 NEW YORK JETS

Pro Football's Undaunted Underdogs

We're going to win on Sunday. I'll guarantee you....

With those words, New York Jet quarterback Joe Namath shocked the football world.

Many who heard Namath make those remarks before the 1969 Super Bowl game against the Baltimore Colts thought he was a loudmouthed braggart. Actually, he was just defending his team against the charge that the Jets were far inferior to the Colts. He got tired of hearing his team put down, so he spoke up. He believed in himself and his teammates, and he said so.

All great teams have the unity of belief and trust. For the Jets, other unique factors contributed to this unity.

They felt they were playing not just for themselves, but for the pride of their league. The Jets were members of the American Football League (AFL), which had been formed in 1960 as a rival to the more established National Football League (NFL). Many of the players in the AFL were those that NFL teams had dismissed as lacking the talent to play in the NFL. The AFL struggled at first, but after nine seasons the AFL's players and management believed their best teams were the equal of those in the NFL. When the Jets faced the Colts in Super Bowl III, they had the whole league rooting for them.

But the Jets were a great team all through the 1968 season, not just before the Super Bowl. One reason for their success was that they had two remarkable leaders—Namath and head coach Weeb Ewbank.

Even those in the NFL admitted that Joe Namath was a superb quarterback and an excellent athlete. His arm was strong enough to throw the ball long, and his short passes were accurate and not too hard for the receivers to catch. But his greatest athletic asset was a quick release when he was passing.

After taking the ball from the center, he would move straight back with choppy tiptoe steps. He would scan the field in front of him, even as 250-pound linemen were rushing in to throw him to the ground. Then he would stop, plant his right foot, cock the ball behind his ear, and fire the ball to the target.

Besides his athletic ability, Namath's mannerisms and style became a trademark for the youth and confidence of the team and the league. As he approached the line for a play, he would hunch his shoulders and slap himself in the chest with an open palm, readying himself for whatever might happen on that play. He wore white shoes on the field and mink coats off the field. His hair was long, and during the 1968 season, he grew a Fu Manchu mustache that a razor company paid him $10,000 to shave on national television.

Weeb Ewbank, the coach and general manager of the team, could not have been more different from Namath in appearance. He was a short, chubby man with hair flattened into a crew cut. He was the man most responsible for choosing and developing the players on the team.

He had been successful as a coach in the NFL, leading the Baltimore Colts for nine seasons and winning two NFL championships. But after the Colts went 7–7 in 1962, Ewbank was fired. He was quickly hired by the Jets.

He began gathering around him the players who would bring him a championship in the AFL. By 1968, that team looked complete. Twenty-seven of the players on that year's **roster** had never played a game for a professional team other than the Jets. Four more were with the team from the days of the previous ownership, when the team was called the Titans. Four others had played for Ewbank when he was coaching the Colts. This familiarity with and loyalty to the team and the coach helped create a calm, confident atmosphere for the Jets before the 1968 season started.

One other unifying factor on the team

TOUCHDOWN TALK

blitz: when the linebackers as well as the defensive linemen pursue the quarterback.
end zone: the ten-yard area past the goal line where touchdowns are scored.
extra point: a kicking play following a touchdown during which the scoring team gets the opportunity to kick the ball from a close range to score a bonus point.
field goal: a three-point score made when the place kicker kicks the ball over the crossbar and through the uprights of the goalpost.
first down: the initial play in a set of four plays during which the offensive team tries to advance the ball ten yards or more; when the offense travels the ten yards in four or fewer plays, the team gets a "first down," that is, another set of four plays to achieve ten yards.
fumble: a ball which a player has firmly in his possession and then loses control of; either team may recover and gain possession of the ball.
interception: a play during which a defensive man catches a ball thrown by the opposing quarterback; the defensive team gains possession of the ball.
pass rush: the pursuit by the defensive line of the opposing quarterback when he is attempting to pass.
punt: a kick in which the ball is dropped and kicked before it hits the ground; usually used to voluntarily give up possession of the ball when a team hasn't achieved a first down.
roster: the complete list of the players on a team.
rushing: the act of moving the ball down the field by a running play after a handoff.
shoestring catch: a play made by a receiver who holds onto a pass which is only inches from hitting the ground.

was, strangely enough, geography. Even though the team was based in New York, it had an unusual number of players with ties to the South on the roster, and a particularly large number from Texas. Of the forty-six players, nine went to college in Texas and eleven others went to college in the South. That's 43 percent of the team. John Dockery, a Jet defensive back from Brooklyn, told Stephen Hanks for the book *The Game That Changed Pro Football*: "I got along with all the guys, even though they seemed like they were from another world. I mean, it seemed like half the team was from Texas. You needed a dictionary and translator to understand those guys."

Three of the offensive ends were from Texas, and they were as good a group as any in pro football. George Sauer, the 6'2" split end from the University of Texas, ran precise patterns and rarely dropped a pass. Don Maynard, a lanky 6'1" 179-pound wide receiver from Texas Western College (now called the University of Texas at El Paso), was speedy and quick, a favorite target of Namath. Second-team receiver Bake Turner was from Texas Tech University and an aspiring country and western singer. Tight end Pete Lammons, the third-leading receiver on the team that season, was a college teammate of Sauer's. Curley Johnson, the team's punter and backup tight end attended the University of Houston.

Two other Jets were University of Texas teammates with Sauer and Lammons: defensive back Jim Hudson and defensive tackle John Elliott. The Lone Star State had many stars on the Jets.

When the season opened, the Jets knew they had some of the most talented players in the AFL, but would they band together as a team? They all knew that the teams with the most talented players don't always win.

The season before, with much of the same talent, the Jets had finished with a record of only 8–5–1. After a strong start that season, powerful running back Emerson Boozer had suffered a knee injury against the Kansas City Chiefs, and the Jets proceeded to drop three straight games. They finished second in their division behind the Houston Oilers.

In the off-season, Boozer needed knee surgery and nobody knew how well he would come back from the injury. He and the other starter at running back, Matt Snell, needed to be healthy if the Jets were to have a balanced **rushing** and passing attack.

A weak rushing game would make Namath more vulnerable to a defensive **pass rush**, when the opposing team attempts to tackle the quarterback as he tries to pass. Namath's injured knees made it difficult for him to escape the rushing defenders.

In the first game of the season, the Jets would face Kansas City, which had one of the fiercest pass rushes in professional football. The four players on Kansas City's defensive line averaged 6'6" and 274 pounds. Even though the game at Kansas City was the first on the schedule, it was an important test for the Jets. They would find out very early in the season just how good they were.

Before the game, the Jets elected Namath the captain of the offensive team. This was a significant gesture. In seasons past, Namath's leadership was sometimes questioned because some players resented his favorable relationship with the team's owner. He was talented, highly paid, and his statistics looked good, but until 1968, Namath's position as a team leader was in doubt. His teammates erased that doubt in everyone's mind by electing him captain.

Namath lived up to his new role in the season opener. The offensive line kept out the Chiefs' defensive pass rush, and Namath was able to complete 17 out of 29 passes for a total of 302 yards. The Jets won 20–19.

Maynard was his favorite receiver of the day, catching eight passes for 203 yards and two touchdowns. Most important of all, the Jets showed they could command the game when necessary. Kansas City kicked a **field goal** to bring them within one point with six minutes remaining. When Kansas City kicked off, the Jet returner went out of bounds at the 5-yard line. With their backs against their own goal, the Jets ran two plays and lost a yard. On the next play, Namath dropped back and passed to Maynard, who was slanting across the middle of the field, for a 16-yard completion and a **first down**. The Jets were out of trouble and were able to run the clock out, saving the victory. Though it was only the first game of the season, it showed that the Jets could protect a lead. That game built their confidence as a team.

The next week, the defensive backfield picked off four passes from Boston Patriot quarterbacks, and Jet placekicker Jim Turner booted four field goals as the Jets won 47–31. In the first two games, the Jets had demonstrated that they had strength in every area. Their passing offense was explosive, the running game was strong, the defensive backfield was crafty, the offensive and defensive lines powerful, and the kicking game solid. Everything was working out as Ewbank had planned.

At least until the Jets traveled to Buffalo. The Buffalo Bills were one of the worst teams in the league. After the first game of the season, which the Bills lost 48–6, their coach was fired. The Jets, going into the game, were expected to win by 20 points. They lost 37–35.

Namath threw four touchdown passes, but he also threw five **interceptions**, three of which the Bills returned for touchdowns. In his first three seasons, Namath had been plagued by interceptions. He had thrown 54 in the 28 games of the two previous seasons. It was his major weakness, and it could kill the team.

After three games on the road, the Jets were happy to return to New York City. There they played their games at Shea Stadium, the home of the New York Mets baseball team. The fans, always a crucial part of team chemistry, saw that the Jets might be good that season and were anxious for them to display their talent at home.

The largest crowd in the nine-year history of the team—63,786 fans—showed up for the game against the undefeated San Diego Chargers. The Chargers were expected to be one of the best teams in the Western Division of the AFL. After his horrendous game the week before, Namath followed Ewbank's game plan of staying on the ground, using the powerful running pair of Boozer and Snell. Of the 74 offensive plays in the game, the Jets ran the ball 40 times and passed 34. In the two previous games, that ratio had been reversed. Namath completed 16 passes for 220 yards, but best of all, he threw no interceptions.

With only 1:43 left in the game, the Jets had a fourth down on the Chargers' 1-yard line. Boozer scored a touchdown on the next play to put the Jets ahead 23–20.

The Chargers still had time to move the ball into position for a score. They drove into the Jet end of the field, but Johnny Sample, a veteran who had played for Ewbank when he was coaching the Colts, intercepted a pass and returned it to midfield with only 29 seconds remaining. The Jets' 23–20 victory was preserved. And equally as important, Namath's confidence returned.

The next week, the Jets were again favored by 20 points over one of the league's weaker teams, the Denver Broncos. Namath's old problem with interceptions arose again, and the Broncos picked off five in a 21–13 upset of the Jets. After the game, Namath said, "I only want to say one thing: I stink."

The Jets had a won-lost record of 3–2. In spite of the two losses, they were getting solid contributions from all areas of the team. Even though they had lost to a couple of the league's worst teams, they had stayed close and had a chance to win the games in the final quarter. Jim Turner was kicking well, and the defense was playing superbly, especially defensive end Gerry Philbin. They forgot about the losses and looked ahead to the next game, an important one with the Houston Oilers, one of their main competitors for the Eastern Division title.

The Jets jumped ahead of the Oilers 13–0 going into the final quarter. The defense had chased Houston's quarterback all day, tackling him for 65 total yards lost. When he went out with an injury, the Jets relaxed and allowed the Oilers to take a 14–13 lead with two quick touchdowns. There were four minutes left in the game.

Namath was faced with the task of leading the Jets down the field for a winning score. An interception in this situation would lose the game for the Jets. Namath threw four straight completions, three to Sauer and one to Boozer, who made a **shoestring catch** to keep the ball from falling incomplete.

On the Oilers' 27-yard line, the Jets turned to their running game. Boozer

After some early-season problems, Namath rallied the Jets to a string of wins.

carried the ball twice and Snell once to take the Jets to the 2-yard line. Snell then followed blocks by linemen Winston Hill and Randy Rasmussen and powered into the end zone to give the Jets the touchdown and the 20–14 win. The Jets had driven 80 yards in three minutes to score the winning touchdown. It was the third time during the season that a long drive had given the Jets a win. The Jets were beginning to show the poise and confidence it takes to be winners.

The next week that confidence grew when the Jets beat the Patriots 48–14 to improve their won-lost record to 5–2 with half the season gone. Another matchup with Buffalo, which had not won a game since beating the Jets early in the season, produced a 25–21 win as Jim Turner kicked a league-record six field goals. The Oilers came to Shea Stadium for a rematch, and the Jets routed them 26–7.

No other team in their division had a winning record, so unless they fell apart as a team, they would be playing for the league championship against the Western Division winner. The next game was against one of the Western Division's leading teams, the Oakland Raiders.

With their black-and-silver uniforms, the Raiders styled themselves the outlaws of the league, playing tough physical football, preferring to overpower rather than outwit their opponents.

The game against the Jets would be one of the strangest and most memorable in football history, though few fans saw the end of it. Late in the fourth quarter, the Jets had a 32–29 lead over the Raiders. Namath had passed for 381 yards, 228 of them to Maynard. He had picked apart the Raider defense all day. The Jets looked like they had the game in control when they kicked off with just 65 seconds remaining.

At that time, the NBC television network decided to interrupt the nationally televised game in order to broadcast the movie *Heidi*, the story of a Swiss orphan girl, as scheduled. In the little time that remained,

the Raiders incredibly scored two touchdowns, when they completed a 43-yard pass in the end zone and when they recovered the **fumbled** kickoff in the **end zone** on the next play. Angry fans jammed the NBC switchboard with calls wondering what had happened to the game. Many fans assumed the Jets had won and didn't find out the truth until they opened their newspapers the next morning.

All the controversy surrounding the broadcast perhaps helped the Jets dismiss the game as a fluke. They won their remaining four games, averaging 32.5 points per game to their opponents' 13.25 points. After they clinched the division title with a win in the first of those four games, the Jets were able to rest key players, using substitutes in the final three games.

The Jets' dedication to team play was evident in that final game when several players had chances to lead the league in statistical categories. Maynard, for one, was in a battle with the Chargers' Lance Alworth for the lead in receiving yardage, or the total yardage covered by all the passes a receiver catches. The Jets' receiver had a slight injury, and rather than risk making the injury worse by playing, he sat out that game and Alworth beat him for the yardage lead by 15 yards. Bake Turner replaced Maynard in the lineup and caught seven passes for 157 yards. Sauer only caught two passes, and Alworth topped him for the league best in number of passes caught, 68 to 66. But the Jets didn't care; they were a team, and they were in the championship game against the Raiders.

On a cold, windy day at the end of December, the Jets and Raiders met in Shea Stadium. The Jets jumped out to a 10–0 lead on a touchdown pass from Namath to Maynard and a 32-yard field goal by Jim Turner. The Raiders struck back with a touchdown pass, then the teams traded field goals, and the Jets led 13–10 at the half.

At the beginning of the third quarter, the Raiders drove down to the Jets' 1-yard line, but the defense held, and Oakland kicked a field goal to tie the game. The Jets answered with an 80-yard drive in fourteen plays, mixing runs and passes so that Oakland never knew what the play was going to be. The last play was a pass to tight end Lammons, who caught the ball on the 5-yard line and bulled between two defenders for the touchdown. The Jets led 20–13 as the fourth quarter began.

After the Raiders drove down for a field goal, the Jets had the ball with nine minutes left. Instead of giving the ball to one of the big running backs to use up time, Namath dropped back to pass and threw to Maynard. Before the ball could get there, the Raiders' George Atkinson stepped in front of Maynard and intercepted the ball at the Jets' 37-yard line. He returned the ball to the Jets' 5-yard line before he was knocked out of bounds by Namath. One play later the Raiders scored to take the lead, 23–20.

The Jets' fans were angry. Why hadn't the Jets just safely run the ball while they had the lead? As Namath and the Jets trotted onto the field after the Raiders kicked off, they were not really worried. All season long, from the first game of the season, they had been able to put together an important drive when they needed it. They needed one now more than any other time during the season.

Starting from the 32-yard line, Namath first fired a 10-yard pass to Sauer. On the next play, he decided to go for the touchdown. Maynard streaked down the right sideline, with the Raiders' Atkinson beside him step for step. Namath hurled the ball downfield. Just before it reached Maynard, who put his hands up in front of his left shoulder to catch it, the wind blew the ball farther right. Maynard adjusted his hands as the ball came over his head, and he caught the ball while leaning to the right. His momentum caused him to run out of bounds at the 6-yard line. It was an amazing catch.

On the next play, Namath found Maynard in the end zone for the touchdown. The Jets were AFL champions and would go to the Super Bowl against the Baltimore Colts. Exactly ten years before, Weeb Ewbank was celebrating his first NFL championship with the Colts.

The AFL-NFL Championship Game wasn't officially named the Super Bowl until the 1969 game. Though the fans and the media had begun calling it that earlier, professional football was slow to adopt the name. In the first two games, the Green Bay Packers overpowered their AFL opponents and fans began to wonder if the quality of football in the AFL would ever make the game worth watching.

The 1969 game seemed unlikely to change that opinion. To many football observers, the 1968-69 Baltimore Colts were one of football's best teams ever. They had suffered only one loss during the season, to the Cleveland Browns, and the Colts had thoroughly routed the Browns in the NFL championship game, 34–0.

In 14 games, the Colts' defense had allowed only 144 points; the Jets' defense had allowed nearly twice that. The defensive line was anchored by two Smiths, Bubba and Billy Ray. Bubba Smith was a giant of a man, standing 6'7" tall and weighing 295 pounds. He was such a feared presence on the line that poet Ogden Nash composed this two-line verse about him:

When hearing tales of Bubba Smith,
You wonder is he man or myth.

On offense, the Colts relied all season on Earl Morrall, a veteran second-string quarterback who had stepped in for the injured great Johnny Unitas and led the Colts to a 13–1 record. He threw 26 touchdown passes and was named the league's Player of the Year. Tight end John Mackey was the leading receiver on the team with 45 catches.

Football writers and oddsmakers had declared that the Jets would lose the game by at least 18 to 20 points. The Jets didn't seem to care. They arrived at their Florida hotel with wives and children in tow, and the players argued with team management about whether they would get rings or watches for winning the AFL championship.

In the intense media coverage leading up to the game, the Colts seemed puzzled about how to respond to the Jets' relaxed, confident attitude. When Namath said that the Colts' Morrall would be only the third-string quarterback on the Jets, his teammate Bubba Smith commented with scorn, "The Green Bay Packers were real champions. They never talked. They never had to. This is the way I visualize all champions: solemn, dignified, humble."

The Jets were anything but that. With all the talk about how badly the Colts were going to beat them, they felt they had to defend themselves. No one was giving them a chance, but they really believed they were a better team than the Colts.

They felt that their strengths matched up well against the Colts' weaknesses. The Colts had a powerful **blitz**, but Namath was one of the best quarterbacks at reading the blitz and adjusting his plays. The Jets also had two of the best blocking backs in football in Boozer and Snell to protect Namath. Jet opponents had tackled Namath in his own backfield only 18 times all year, the fewest in the league.

Watching films convinced the Jets that the Colts were not as strong as everyone was making them out to be. They had won a lot of games when they recovered fumbles or intercepted passes, and the Jets were convinced that they could control the ball against them and not make those mistakes.

By the afternoon of January 12, 1969, all the talk was over. The teams lined up for the opening kickoff. Only the play on the field would determine which was the better team: the flashy, brash, young New York Jets or the serious, veteran Baltimore Colts.

After the Jets were forced to punt during their first series, the Colts took over the ball and immediately began moving it with ease. Morrall passed to Mackey for 19 yards. Two more first downs from the Colt running backs took the ball down to the Jets' 36-yard line. Morrall passed again, and with just over five and a half minutes left in the first quarter, the Colts were on the Jets' 19-yard line. Morrall dropped back to pass three times. Twice his passes fell incomplete, and the Colts went nowhere. Colt kicker Lou Michaels came on to try a field goal, but the 27-yard attempt went wide.

After the Jets failed to advance past their own 41-yard line, they **punted**, and the Colts could do no better, running only three plays before they had to punt.

Just before the end of the first quarter, Namath, deep in his own territory, completed a pass to Sauer, who fumbled the ball, which was recovered by the Colts. Though the quarter ended with the game tied at zero, the Colts surely wouldn't get that close twice in a row without scoring. The Jets' defense tightened. Two plays later, Baltimore was on the New York 6-yard line. Morrall dropped back to pass, spotted Tom Mitchell in the end zone and fired the ball. Jet defensive back Al Atkinson tipped it just enough to change the course of the pass. The ball hit Mitchell on the shoulder pads and shot up into the air, where Jet defensive back Randy Beverly caught and cradled it for the interception.

The Colts appeared stunned. Twice they had moved down inside the Jet 20-yard line and had failed to score. Jet defensive back Bill Baird said in *The Game That Changed Pro Football*: "Panic started to set in on their side early."

With a new surge of confidence, the Jets took the ball at their own 20-yard line. The Colts had heard so much about Namath's passing ability that they were surprised when he handed the ball off to his backs four straight times to the left, gaining a total of 26 yards. When they adjusted to that, Namath went to the air, passing four

Strong Jet blocking sprung Matt Snell for a
121-yard rush against the Colts.

straight times and completing three downs to the Baltimore 23-yard line. He was keeping the Colts guessing whether he would run or pass next.

Four plays later from the 4-yard line, Snell, running again to the left where the Jets had run successfully earlier in the drive, pounded over for the touchdown. With the **extra point**, the Jets led 7–0. The Colt fans were silent, while the Jet fans erupted.

After each side missed a long field goal, Baltimore got the ball back, and running back Tom Matte exploded off the right side for 58 yards to the Jets' 16-yard line. Once again the Jets came up with a big defensive play. Morrall dropped back to throw, and when he missed his receiver, Jet defensive back Johnny Sample, the former Colt, stepped in and intercepted it. For the third time in the first half, the Colts had been stopped without a score inside the Jets' 20.

Baltimore had one more chance before the half ended. With 20 seconds left, the Colts tried a trick play: Morrall handed off to Matte, who threw the ball back to Morrall, who then looked downfield for a receiver. Split end Jimmy Orr was wide open, waving his arms in the end zone, but Morrall didn't see him and instead threw the ball over the middle where the Jets intercepted it.

FOOTBALL POSITIONS

Offense

quarterback: the player who directs the offensive team by handing the ball to another player, passing it, or keeping it himself.

running back: usually one of two players positioned behind the quarterback; he may take the ball from the quarterback on a running play, receive a pass, or block oncoming defensive players.

offensive linemen: the five players who form the front wall of the offensive team and who are mainly responsible for keeping opposing players away from the quarterback. The linemen include the **center**, who plays in the middle of the line and starts each play by passing the ball through his legs to the quarterback; two **guards**, on either side of the center; and two **tackles**, positioned on the other side of each guard.

ends: players positioned on the ends of the line and who have the ability to catch passes. The different types of ends include the **tight end**, who usually plays close to the tackle and is used both as a blocker and a pass catcher, and the **split end**, also sometimes called a **wide receiver**, whose primary responsibility is to catch passes.

Defense

defensive linemen: the front line of the defensive team, these players attempt to fight off the blocks of the offensive linemen and other players to tackle the player with the ball.

linebackers: these players are positioned just behind the linemen and are responsible for covering offensive players who go downfield to catch a pass or who get past the linemen on a running play.

defensive backs: the main duty of these players, who are positioned behind the linebackers, is to stay close to opposing players who go downfield in order to catch a pass.

Kickers

punter: when the offensive team has stalled after a series of plays, he transfers the ball to the opposing team by dropping it and kicking it before the ball hits the ground.

place kicker: he attempts to score by kicking the ball (balanced on the ground by a teammate) through the uprights and over the crossbar of the goalposts.

The half ended with the Jets ahead, 7–0.

The chemistry of a team can change even during a game. Teams that played with confidence all year can see belief fade in a matter of minutes. That seemed to be happening to Baltimore.

The first play of the second half confirmed how flustered the Colts had become. Matte tried a run off the right side of the line and fumbled. The Jets recovered.

Snell kept running off the Colts' vulnerable left side, and when the offense stalled at the Baltimore 25-yard line, Jim Turner came in and kicked a 32-yard field goal. The score was 10–0.

On the next series, the Jets held the Colts to three plays before a punt. Once again the Jets were able to move the ball on the Colt defense. Namath hit four passes that took the Jets into Colt territory for another field goal. The score was 13–0.

The Colts were still not out of it. In spite of the Jets' dominance, two touchdowns and two extra points would put Baltimore ahead. The Jets had seen the Raiders score two TDs in nine seconds in the "Heidi" game, so they knew what could happen.

Ever since the Kansas City game that opened the season, the Jets knew they could control the ball when they had to. Taking the ball at their own 37-yard line, they marched down the field, with Namath mixing runs and passes expertly. On a crucial third-down play from their own 40-yard line, he completed a pass to Sauer for a first down and followed that with a 39-

Jim Turner's four field goals provided the margin of victory in Super Bowl III.

yard completion to Sauer. Then the Jets stalled at the Baltimore 2-yard line, but Jim Turner booted the 9-yard field goal and the Jets went up 16–0. The Colts would have to score three times to win the game.

Baltimore rallied for a touchdown behind Unitas, who had replaced Morrall late in the third quarter. Unitas was not the quarterback he had once been. His passes lacked the snap they had once possessed, and he lacked the magic to rescue the Colts. All the magic that day belonged to Namath and his teammates. The scoreboard read "Jets 16, Colts 7" as the final seconds ticked off the clock.

Joe Namath trotted off the field, a big smile on his face and his index finger in the air, signaling "No. 1." As they made their way to the locker room, Jet guard Dave Herman approached Namath and said, "You told the truth, Joe."

FOR THE EXTRA POINT

Aaseng, Nathan. *Football's Super Bowl Champions: I-VIII*. Minneapolis: Lerner, 1982.

Aaseng, Nathan. *Football: You Are the Coach.* Minneapolis: Lerner, 1983.

Aaseng, Nathan. *Football's Most Shocking Upsets.* Minneapolis: Lerner, 1985.

Anderson, Dave. *Countdown to Super Bowl.* New York: Random House, 1969. (Advanced readers.)

Brenner, Richard. *The Complete Super Bowl Story: Games I-XXIII*. Minneapolis: Lerner, 1989.

Hanks, Stephen. *The Game That Changed Pro Football*. New York: Birch Lane Press, 1989. (Advanced readers.)

Namath, Joe, and Dick Schaap. *I Can't Wait Until Tomorrow Cause I Get Better Looking Every Day*. New York: Random House, 1969. (Advanced readers.)

1968–69 NEW YORK JETS

SUPER BOWL STATISTICS

Team	1st	2nd	3rd	4th	Final
New York Jets	0	7	6	3	16
Baltimore Colts	0	0	0	7	7

Scoring Summary

Team	Quarter	Description of Scoring Play	Score
New York	2nd	Snell, 4-yard run, Turner kick	7–0
New York	3rd	Turner, 32-yard field goal	10–0
New York	3rd	Turner, 30-yard field goal	13–0
New York	4th	Turner, 9-yard field goal	16–0
Baltimore	4th	Hill, 1-yard run, Michaels kick	16–7

SUPER BOWL STATISTICS

Individual Statistics

Rushing

Team	Player	Attempts	Yards	Touchdowns
New York	Snell	30	121	1
	Boozer	10	19	0
	Mathis	3	2	0
	Totals	43	142	1
Baltimore	Matte	11	116	0
	Hill	9	29	1
	Morrall	2	-2	0
	Unitas	1	0	0
	Totals	23	143	1

Passing

Team	Player	Attempts/Complete		Yds.	TDs	Interceptions
New York	Namath	28	17	206	0	0
	Parilli	1	0	0	0	0
	Totals	29	17	206	0	0
Baltimore	Morrall	17	6	71	0	3
	Unitas	24	11	110	0	1
	Totals	41	17	181	0	4

Receiving

Team	Player	Receptions	Yds.	TDs
New York	Sauer	8	133	0
	Snell	4	40	0
	Mathis	3	20	0
	Lammons	2	13	0
	Totals	17	206	0
Baltimore	Richardson	6	58	0
	Orr	3	42	0
	Mackey	3	35	0
	Matte	2	30	0
	Hill	2	1	0
	Mitchell	1	15	0
	Totals	17	181	0

Torvill and Dean practiced for hours to achieve a seemingly effortless grace.

JAYNE TORVILL & CHRISTOPHER DEAN

Ice Dancing's Perfect Pair

Before they met each other early one morning in 1975 at an ice rink in Nottingham, England, Jayne Torvill and Christopher Dean were fine skaters. They had won a few competitions with other partners, but nothing they had done to that point led them to believe that they could be the best in the world, the best ever.

Then they skated *together*. The transformation into a team did not happen all at once. There were arguments, disappointments, mistakes, and falls to the ice. There were early mornings and late nights of training at deserted rinks. But in time they began to glide over the ice together as no one had before them. The two skaters seemed to move as one.

Jayne Torvill and Christopher Dean were both born in Nottingham, England, a city of 300,000 located in the center of the country. Raleigh bicycles are made there, but the city is perhaps best known as part of the area haunted by Robin Hood, the outlaw-hero who stole from the rich and gave to the poor.

Torvill was born in October 1957. Her parents ran a newspaper and magazine store, and the family lived in an apartment above the shop. One day when she was nine years old, a teacher took her to an ice rink, and she began to learn to skate.

Dean was born in July 1958, and his family was also one of modest income. His father was an electrician. Dean began skating at the age of ten when his mother encouraged him to take up an after-school activity. His family further fueled his interest by giving him a pair of ice skates for Christmas. Early on in his career Dean crashed into a rink barrier and broke his leg. But he was determined to come back from his injury and excel at the sport.

Both Torvill and Dean achieved some early success individually and with other partners. At age twelve, Torvill won the British junior pairs figure skating championship with Michael Hutchinson, and the two finished second in the senior pairs championship that same year. The next year, still with Hutchinson as her partner, they won the British senior pairs.

Dean was always involved in ice dancing rather than figure skating. In 1974, he won the British junior ice dancing championship with a skater named Sandra Elson.

Figure skating and ice dancing are related but separate events contested on an ice rink. Figure skating has a longer and more prestigious history. It has been an official Olympic event since 1908. Skaters compete individually in men's or women's events or as a male and female pair. Such American stars as Dick Button, Peggy Fleming, Dorothy Hamill, Scott Hamilton and Brian Boitano won Olympic gold medals in individual competition.

Comparing ice dancing with the better-known sport of pairs figure skating emphasizes some of the major differences between the two. In pairs competition, there were formerly two sections on which the skaters are judged. One section, the "compulsories" (which was eliminated as of 1990) required the pair to perform certain specific sequences of moves. In the other section, the "freestyle," the pair is largely unlimited in its choice of movement; the only restriction is for the skaters to give an impression of unity and harmony. During the competition, pairs engage in spectacular lifts, spins, jumps, and throws. Sometimes the male skater will lift the female high above his head or perform other acrobatic maneuvers.

Skaters in ice dancing have many more restrictions than those in pairs. They have their own set of compulsories, which consist of famous dance steps performed on the ice. There are four groups of three compulsory dances each. During the annual skating season, two of those groups are designated by skating's governing body to be used for the year. Before each competition, the judges pick one of the two groups for the skating pairs to execute. Altogether, the skaters have to know twelve complex steps: the Viennese, Westminster, starlight, and Ravensburger waltzes, the yankee polka, the blues, the paso doble, the rumba, the kilian, the tango romantica, the quickstep, and the Argentine tango. Their performance in this segment counts for 30 percent of their total score.

Next comes the "original set pattern," a two-minute routine of a dance, predetermined by competition officials.

The showcase of the competition is the free dance routine, which is actually not so free, considering all the limitations that apply. The skaters' four-minute routine must include at least three rhythm changes. They must never be separated on the ice for more than five seconds or farther than two arm lengths. While pairs skaters design their programs to include some easy moves to prepare them for strenuous lifts and throws, the ice dancers aren't able to do that because of the rules of their routines.

At the present time, ice dancers are not allowed to perform jumps during which they turn more than half a full rotation, or, in other words, 180 degrees. They can't turn somersaults, nor are they permitted to perform any lifts where the man's arms rise above his shoulders. This keeps the competition truer to its name—dancing—than to the gymnastics of figure skating.

Ice dancing originated in Great Britain in the 1930s and has sometimes been treated as a poor sister to figure skating. After years of campaigning, the International Skating Union, skating's governing body, persuaded the International Olympic Committee to adopt the sport as part of the Winter Olympics. Ice dancing made its first Olympic appearance as an exhibition sport in 1968 and became an official event for the first time in 1976.

The pair's *Barnum on Ice* program re-created the acts in a three-ring circus.

Competitors in both events must have extraordinary grace, strength, stamina, and flexibility. In ice dancing, nine judges score the skaters up to 6.0 in two categories, technical merit and artistic impression. In international events each judge is from a different country.

Torvill and Dean have revolutionized their sport by taking advantage of one of the most loosely defined rules of ice dancing: the requirement that the couple must "interpret" the music to which they are dancing. Their interpretations always seem one step ahead of everybody else's.

They first came together in 1975, when they found themselves without partners at the Nottingham rink. Though they had enjoyed some success in national competitions, they didn't know how much further they could go, or even if each was the right partner for the other. They agreed to a one-month trial to see if they were suited for each other on the ice. After a month, they agreed to try it for two more months. Soon they discovered that they both had an almost fanatical devotion to skating that bordered on obsession.

Feeding an obsession is difficult when you are holding a full-time job. Dean was a member of the Nottingham police force, and Torvill was working as a clerk in an insurance office. Because of their jobs, they had to schedule training either early in the morning or late at night when the rink was closed to the public. Occasionally, they didn't close up the place until four in the morning.

Under the direction of their coach, Janet Sawbridge, they began to rise slowly to the top of the British ice dancing ladder. After winning a number of local and regional titles, the pair placed fourth in the British Championship in 1976 and third the next year. After they won the British Championship and finished ninth in the European Championship in 1978, Betty Callaway became their trainer.

An ice dancer since the early days of the sport, Callaway had been an independent coach and trainer for eighteen years before becoming the West German national coach in 1971. With her guidance, Torvill and Dean kept improving. They won the British Championship in 1979, moved up to sixth in the European, and finished eighth in the World Championship.

They traveled to Lake Placid, New York, for the 1980 Winter Olympics, and on the same rink where the American Olympic hockey team won its gold medal, they skated to a fifth-place finish. They were just beginning to realize what they could do. But they couldn't do more until they bought some more time.

The Soviet Union was the dominant country in the sport, and its government supported its skaters financially, allowing them to devote their full time to skating. If Torvill and Dean were to hope to compete

at the international level, they would have to quit their jobs and devote more time to their sport. It was not an easy decision. Unemployment in Great Britain was high, and giving up a good job was not wise. They had saved enough money to support themselves for six months, but beyond that....

Coming from working-class families, they couldn't turn to their parents for help. They worked out a budget that would cover expenses to take them to the 1984 Olympics in Sarajevo, Yugoslavia. Shopping around for a sponsor, they found help at home. In the tradition of Robin Hood giving to the poor, the Nottingham City Council, over the objections of some members, voted them a grant of £14,000 (approximately $21,000) per year for three years. The Sports Aid Foundation, a British athletic support organization, added £8,000 to that, and the couple could then concentrate on their artistry instead of their pocketbooks.

The money allowed them to train with Callaway at the West German training site at Oberstdorf, which has some of the best facilities in the world. The payoff was almost immediate. They won the European title in 1981. Callaway told London's *Sunday Times Magazine*: "Once they were free to devote all their time to training, they quickly matured and acquired the polish and personality they had been lacking before."

Next they competed in the World Championships in Hartford, Connecticut. During their free program, they showed remarkable variety by skating a quick-step to the song "Hot Lunch Jam" from the movie *Fame*, a specialty dance to the jazz classic "Caravan," a slow rumba to the standard "Red Sails in the Sunset," and a jaunty closing dance to the song "Swing, Swing, Swing." With the completion of that program came victory in the World Championships.

What could they do to improve? They couldn't improve on first-place finishes, but they could start inching their scores closer and closer to perfection. And that's exactly what they did. At the 1982 World Championships in Copenhagen, Denmark, their final routine earned five 6.0s for artistic expression from the nine judges.

For their successes in 1981 and 1982, the British Sports Writers' Association voted them Team of the Year twice.

But no one in any form of skating equalled what the duo accomplished at the 1983 World Championships. They were the favored team going into the competition in Helsinki, Finland. When they unveiled their four-minute free dance program at the World Championships, the fans, the other competitors, and the judges saw an astounding performance. The program was called *Barnum on Ice*, with songs taken from the hit New York and London musical *Barnum*, which was based on the life of circus producer and showman P.T. Barnum.

Dean, who is the principal choreographer of the routines for the pair, had gotten the idea for a circus theme when he visited the Moscow State Circus on a trip to Russia in 1982. He and Torvill had worked on it for a year.

The show on the ice was nothing less than a three-ring circus mimed by two people. The skaters imitated clowns, tightrope walkers, trombone players,

The dramatic falling finish of Torvill and Dean's *Bolero* earned them a standing ovation.

jugglers, tumblers, and trapeze artists. They glided over the ice effortlessly, creating the world of Barnum.

In doing so, they challenged the rules and limitations of their sport. Torvill told *Sports Illustrated*: "The rules say no acrobatics, but, after all, we're doing a *circus* number, and the rules also say that we must interpret the music." Would the judges reward them or penalize them for taking chances, for pushing the limits?

When they finished their performance, the technical merit scores flashed up first. One after the other, judge after judge, the numbers appeared: 5.9, 5.9, 5.9 until nine of them were standing in a row.

Then for artistic impression, again the numbers lighted on the scoreboard, but this time, the row was glowing with nine 6.0s. A perfect score! Never before in the history of skating had a routine earned nine perfect scores! The scores gave Torvill and Dean their third World Championship in a row.

The only title left for Torvill and Dean to conquer was perhaps the most sought after, the Olympic gold medal. They had reached their peak just after the 1980 Olympics. Would they still be the best in the world in 1984? Had their triumph at the 1983 World Championships been the best they could do? How could they top perfection?

But first, how did they achieve perfection?

For a team like Torvill and Dean flawlessness does not arrive without devoting countless hours to training. As effortless and smooth as their movements appear on the ice, that look of ease is deceptive. Hours and hours of practice have preceded the competition in which a difficult move looks simple. Callaway told *Sports Illustrated*, "Only by constant repetition year after year can you finally get it right. Some skaters never do..." Dean has said, "We've adapted to one another. We spend more time together— maybe eight or ten hours a day—than many husbands and wives."

With the time spent together comes a complete knowledge of where the partner is and what he or she should be doing at any moment on the ice. If there is a change in the position of one or the other, they are aware of it. Dean told *The Christian Science Monitor*: "If Jayne's eye level isn't right or if her body is an inch out of place, I know it." Callaway has said, "This is a *couple* performing, not a pair." If one of them makes a mistake during a routine, the other will mirror it so that it looks as if it were a planned move.

But when Torvill and Dean take the ice, what they create is more than just cooperation and coordination. People don't just admire the way they skate; fans lose themselves in the emotions that the skaters create, in the story that they tell with their dancing. Dean told *The Washington Post*, "We go into a fantasy world when we step onto the ice, and we want people to believe it as well."

As the 1984 Olympics neared, they prepared a program they hoped would be their best ever. At Sarajevo, the fantasy that Torvill and Dean created was a tale of doomed love. Using the music of *Bolero*, a classical piece written by French composer Maurice Ravel, their dancing told the tale of two lovers who throw themselves into the crater of a live volcano because they cannot be together. In the months preceding the Olympics, they worked non-stop on the routine.

Before the Olympics British officials were so proud of the pair, they wanted to have both Torvill and Dean carry the British flag together for the parade of nations during the opening ceremonies in Sarajevo. Unfortunately Olympic rules would not allow two people that privilege, and Dean had to carry it by himself.

But they were reunited for the compulsory part of the competition. The pair scored three perfect sixes from the nine judges in the dance called the Westminster waltz. It was another record-

Gold medals, flowers, and perfect scores followed the pair's 1984 Olympic performance.

breaking performance, the first time ever a perfect score had been awarded in Olympic competition for a compulsory dance. They were comfortably in first place.

In the original set pattern dance, a difficult Spanish circular step called the *paso doble*, Torvill and Dean showed that they were human. Their routine included a move called a "death drop," in which Torvill falls backward nearly to the ice while Dean supports her with his hand on her neck. While she is almost parallel to the ice, he sweeps her around in a circle. The move takes strength on his part and trust on hers. The first two times they brought off the move flawlessly, but the third time, Torvill lost her balance slightly and touched her hand to the ice. They didn't lose many points for the error, but their lead had been reduced so that a second-place finish in the free dance could result in a second place overall.

As it happened, the free dance routine was scheduled for Valentine's Day, and Torvill and Dean's romantic *Bolero* was perfect for that day.

Back in Great Britain, an estimated fifteen million television viewers were tuned in to the performance.

Wearing purple costumes that took six months to make, the skaters began the routine on their knees in a simulated embrace. Dean then picked up Torvill and slid her over his shoulder onto the ice.

He then demonstrated his flexibility when he performed a full split with body twists. At one point during the four-minute tragedy of lost love, Dean lifted Torvill off the ice with his free leg, a surprising move that drew prolonged applause from the capacity crowd.

Finally, the performance built to a striking finish in which Dean swung Torvill into the imaginary mouth of the volcano. He followed, and they both ended the routine by falling to the ice. The audience, however, jumped to its feet in a standing ovation.

The couple waited for the judges to make their decisions. First came the marks for technical merit. Six 5.9s and three 6.0s flashed on the scoreboard.

Would they be able to equal that string of perfect 6.0s for artistic merit that they had received the year before at the World Championships?

The numbers appeared above the ice: 6.0, 6.0, 6.0, 6.0, 6.0, 6.0, 6.0, 6.0, 6.0! Nine perfect scores again! The gold medal was theirs.

Unlike the flag-carrying in the opening parade, Olympic rules could not separate them for the medal ceremony. They stood on the platform together.

FOR THE EXTRA POINT

Torvill, Jane and Christopher Dean with John Hennessy. *Torvill & Dean*. New York: St. Martin's Press, 1983. (Advanced readers.)

JAYNE TORVILL AND CHRISTOPHER DEAN

ICE DANCING CHAMPIONSHIPS

British Champions: 1978, 1979, 1980, 1981, 1982, 1983
European Champions: 1981, 1982, 1984
World Champions: 1981, 1982, 1983, 1984
Olympic Champions: 1984

NUMBER OF MAXIMUMS
(6.0 SCORE GIVEN BY JUDGE)

Year	Competition	Place	Description of Score
1981	British Championships	Nottingham, England	7 out of possible 9
1982	European Championships	Lyon, France	11 for free routine
1982	World Championships	Copenhagen, Denmark	5 for artistic impression in final routine
1983	World Championships	Helsinki, Finland	9 out of 9 for presentation in *Barnum* routine
1984	European Championships	Budapest, Hungary	11 for free routine
1984	Olympic Games	Sarajevo, Yugoslavia	19 for three routines
1984	World Championships	Ottawa, Canada	29 total

Very different on land, Ruiz and Costie strove to be identical in water.

CANDY COSTIE AND TRACIE RUIZ

A Matched Set

Candy Costie and Tracie Ruiz are different in hair color, complexion, and personality, but when they teamed up to compete in the sport of synchronized swimming, they were identical. In fact, that is the object of the sport. The swimmers must complete a complicated series of movements in exactly the same way.

Like sports such as figure skating, ice dancing, and gymnastics, synchronized swimming combines athletic ability with artistic creativity. The duet event in the sport—there are also solo and team events—adds the dimension of cooperation to those aspects. The word synchronize means "to operate in unison," and Costie and Ruiz worked together for ten years to insure that every move one of them made in the water was perfectly matched by the other.

Just as some people have a difficult time thinking of ice dancers like Torvill and Dean as athletes, synchronized swimming has had to overcome a glamorous public image to get people to take it seriously as a sport. A name change helped. The sport used to be called "water ballet," and many of its moves are similar to dance steps. In 1934, the name "synchronized swimming" first came into use, reportedly by a radio announcer who was trying to describe for his listeners what the sport looked like.

Some of the early pioneers of the sport became movie stars. The most famous was a woman named Esther Williams who, before taking up synchronized swimming, was the American 100-meter freestyle swimming champion. She made several movies during the 1940s and 1950s that were called "water spectacles" and bore names like *Million Dollar Mermaid*. The films featured Williams along with a cast of hundreds of other swimmers performing dives and swimming moves in unison. People thought of the skills Williams displayed merely as entertainment, but actually they took great athletic skill to perform.

Some of the elements of Hollywood entertainment still endure in the sport. A synchronized swimming competition is divided into two parts: the "figures," during which a swimmer demonstrates her mastery of certain required moves in the water; and the "routine," which is a choreographed combination of moves performed to music as in figure skating or gymnastics. During the routine, the swimmers wear colorful, specially designed suits, sometimes adorned with sequins or other frills. Much of the action of the routine is under water, and music is piped in through speakers located both above ground and under the water so the swimmers can hear it at all times. They also wear makeup and bright smiles.

While Williams was swimming across the screen in movie theaters, synchronized swimming was developing more legitimately as a sport. In 1945, the Amateur Athletic Union adopted it as an official sport, and in 1948, it was included in the Olympics as a demonstration sport. The 1984 Games in Los Angeles marked synchronized swimming's first appearance there as an official sport.

By the time the sport was accepted by the International Olympic Committee, Costie and Ruiz had already been working for years to become the best. Both began swimming at an early age for different swimming clubs in the Seattle, Washington, area.

When they were both eleven, the clubs merged into the Seattle Aqua Club, and their partnership was formed. Their coach was Charlotte Davis, a former junior national duet champion (with Diann Smith) in 1968. Costie and Ruiz worked so well together that Davis told them they eventually had a chance to be national champions.

They continued to work hard, and in 1978, Davis thought they were good enough to travel to Hawaii to compete in a regional meet. There was one problem. Davis couldn't afford the airfare to go with them, and their parents were spending all they could afford to foot the bills for the girls.

Neither came from a wealthy family. Ruiz's mother was a secretary and her stepfather a machinist. Costie's father worked for the phone company, and her mother was a bookkeeper. Their parents decided that, though they were only thirteen, they had earned the right to go, even without a chaperon or coach. The girls justified their parents' confidence in them by coming home with a sixth-place award.

Together only three years, Costie and Ruiz improved enough to become the best in their age-group in the country. They won the National Junior Olympic title in 1977 and 1978. But those successes were not achieved without hardships or disagreements.

Their training schedule left little time for other activities. They would be up before dawn for two hours of practice before school. After school, they would spend another hour in the pool. On the weekends, five hours a day devoted to training.

Spending so much time together was bound to result in some friction. They had fights, as good friends often do, but the disagreements never lasted. The rivalry had even benefited their performance as a team, according to Ruiz. She told *Women's Sports* magazine, "It keeps you working, knowing the other person with you in the pool is the other top competitor in the world."

While competing together in the duet, the pair also competed against each other in solo events. Costie was stronger in solo until age fifteen, then Ruiz began beating her. Costie eventually resigned herself to Ruiz's skill as a solo swimmer. "I decided that I could either be a poor second in solo," Costie told *Sports Illustrated* magazine, "or I could hold up my end. You can't have two people on top." Unless

During some routines, the pair remained under water for nearly a minute.

those two are members of a team.

Watching a soloist twist, turn, and leap in the water may be impressive, but when two swimmers execute identical moves, the performance is even more powerful. Costie and Ruiz created something together that neither could have done alone. Davis has said of them: "They have sort of a charisma when swimming together. They're able to reach out to the crowd or the judges and draw them into the routine."

In the pool, the two were mirror images. Out of the pool, they were very different people. In personality, Costie was talkative and outgoing, while Ruiz was shy and reserved. Though they were the same height (5'4"), Costie was blonde with fair skin, while Ruiz had dark hair and a dark complexion. In a sport where the judges score a routine for the exact images it contains, swimmers who look as different as Costie and Ruiz are at a disadvantage. In fact, some of the top teams in the world are twin sisters. To minimize the dissimilarities, Costie and Ruiz fixed their hair and makeup in the same fashion before a competition.

Preparing their faces and hair for a routine was a time-consuming task. First, they put their hair in a bun on the top of the head. Then they prepared a bowl of unflavored gelatin to smooth onto their hair, making it look shiny in the water. Uniform hats were pinned around the bun, and makeup was applied to the face.

What Costie and Ruiz lacked in physical likeness, they made up for in perfectly matched moves. By 1981, the two eighteen-year-olds were dominating national and even international competitions. They won the duets at the National Sports Festival, the U.S. Championships, and the Pan Pacific Championships.

When the two graduated from high school, their success won them a pair of athletic scholarships to attend the University of Arizona and join the school's synchronized swimming team. During their freshman year they were invited to the Moscow Invitational, the first-ever synchronized swimming meet to be held in the Soviet Union. Against some of the best teams in the world, Costie and Ruiz won the duet.

When they returned home, they quickly prepared for the national collegiate championship, which they also won. Then it was off to Guayaquil, Ecuador, for the 1982 World Championships, the largest and most competitive meet in the world.

The main rivals for Costie and Ruiz were Sharon Hambrook and Kelly Kryczka of Canada. Their specialty was the figures portion of the competition. These measure the technical skill of the synchronized swimmer in the water. There are six groups

The pair's smiles, as well as their perfectly mirrored movements, impressed the judges.

of figures, each with six moves; one of those groups is selected at random by a panel of judges before the competition starts. A swimmer must know thirty-six moves in all, but only has to perform six at any one meet.

The figures have names like "Eiffel Tower," "dolphin," and "barracuda." In a barracuda, for example, the swimmer, lying flat on her back on top of the water, flips her legs (with knees locked) into the air over her head in a backward somersault. Now completely submerged, she completes the rotation and thrusts her legs straight up out of the water until the surface of the water is at her hips. Then straightening her torso under the water, she lowers her legs below the surface, straight down like the periscope of a submarine. In the figures, the judges look for timing and control, then they score the swimmer on a ten-point scale.

Even in the duet, the teammates must complete the figures individually and be judged separately. They perform in black bathing suits, in contrast to the flashy suits many synchronized swimmers use for their "routine" portion of the competition. The teammates' scores for the figures are averaged together to get the total team score—usually in the 90s for the top teams—for that part of the competition. The score in the figures counts 50 percent of the final total in determining the winner.

As it happened, in Guyaquil the figures selected were the ones that gave Costie and Ruiz the most trouble. Ruiz completed the figures in good shape, but Costie finished 23rd overall. The Canadian team of Hambrook and Kryczka took the lead with 92.54 points. Although Costie and Ruiz won the routine portion that followed, their score was not high enough to overtake the Canadians for first place. They finished second. It was the first time in a long time that Costie and Ruiz had not come out on top.

Costie knew that she would have to improve in the figures if they were to have a chance of beating Hambrook and Kryczka at the Olympics in Los Angeles. Though that was two years away, Costie and Ruiz were already anticipating a rematch.

They decided to take a leave of absence from their studies at Arizona in order to move back home to Washington and train for the Olympics under Davis. Soon they were working out 35 to 40 hours a week. They swam underwater laps to increase the amount of time they could hold their breath. (One time a television interviewer asked Ruiz to hold her breath for as long as she could; she did it for 2 minutes and 25 seconds.) Weight lifting for strength also became part of their training, as well as running to improve stamina and dance classes to make them more flexible.

In synchronized swimming, the competitors are not allowed to touch the bottom or sides of the pool, so they have to master a circular underwater kicking motion called the "eggbeater," which is used in water polo. The kick allows them to stay high above the surface of the water, but it takes great stamina to sustain it.

Most of all, Costie and Ruiz enjoyed the creative part of the sport, planning their routine. They chose the music and worked out new maneuvers, either acting them out on land or drawing them in a sketchbook before using them in the water.

They got back on the winning track in 1983 with victories at the National Sports Festival, the U.S. Championships (their third straight national title), and the Pan American Games. After winning the Olympic Trials in 1984, they earned the right to represent the United States in the Olympics.

The preliminaries of the duet routine were the first synchronized swimming event in Los Angeles. There was a sellout crowd of 12,000 on hand. In fact, all the tickets for the synchronized swimming events had sold out almost immediately. From the preliminaries, the eight highest-scoring

At the 1984 Olympics, the team's final routine brought the crowd to its feet.

teams would go on to the finals, where they would perform their routines again.

When Costie and Ruiz completed their routine, the judges penalized them a point because, the judges said, they were short of the 3 minute 45 second minimum time. The Americans couldn't understand what had happened. They had timed their routine over and over again in practice, and it had always been well over the minimum. When the day's competition ended, because of the penalty, they found themselves in second place behind the Canadian team of Hambrook and Kryczka.

Later, an error was discovered. The official timer had started the clock when the pair entered the water instead of when the music started, as the rules state. The mistake was corrected, the penalty was lifted, and Costie and Ruiz assumed first place.

Two days later, the swimmers gathered again at the Olympic Swim Stadium for the figures. The judges, by pure coincidence, chose the group of figures that Costie had performed so poorly at the World Championships two years before. This time she was ready. She had lost 22 pounds since then and was much more confident in all her moves. After the five-hour session was over, Costie finished fifth overall with a score of 93.700. Ruiz led the field with a total of 99.467. Their average in the figures was 96.584. The Canadian swimmers, Hambrook and Kryczka, finished third and fourth respectively, and turned in a team average of 96.034.

Ruiz commented, "It's the hardest group for us, and this has been a nervous day. But this is the best we've ever done. We just wanted to stay close to the Canadians."

So it all came down to the final routine.

The Canadians and the Americans would battle it out for the gold medal, the first one ever awarded in their sport.

The Canadians were up first. Their style displayed a flashy athleticism which drew from the Hollywood tradition of synchronized swimming. Toward the end of their routine, they performed the last of three spectacular lifts and finished to the playful sound of "Rock Around the Clock." It was a rousing performance, and the crowd rewarded them with an ovation. The judges were also impressed and gave the team a total of 98.2 points.

Costie and Ruiz, the last duet to perform, knew they would have to give their best effort. They needed a score of 97.7 or better to win the gold. From the moment they entered the pool, they demonstrated boldness and strength, performing the first 50 seconds of their routine with their heads under water. At one point, a submerged Costie lifted Ruiz completely out of the water by her shoulders, so that Ruiz appeared to be standing on her head on the surface. They won the crowd over with a couple of moves adapted from break dancing and finished with a patriotic salute as "Yankee Doodle Dandy" blared from the speakers. They added that song just for the Olympics, and it brought the predominantly American crowd to its feet, clapping and cheering. But had the routine impressed the judges, too?

The judges entered their scores, and when the numbers were tallied up, Costie and Ruiz were awarded 99.0 points. They won! After all the years of hard work, they finally wore the gold medals around their necks. Reaching that goal, they decided they had accomplished all they could together and ended their partnership.

After the medal ceremony, the reactions of the two teammates—to their win and to their parting—reflected the differences in their personalities. Ruiz had tears in her eyes at the thought of all that she and Costie had accomplished. "I don't know whether I'm happy or sad," said Ruiz. "I mean I do know. I'm both. All the years we've spent together...." She began to cry harder. "We're like sisters. I know we'll always stay in touch."

Costie was beaming from ear to ear. "Knowing that we couldn't have worked any harder makes it extra special," she said. "And winning it with Tracie makes it extra, extra special."

CANDY COSTIE AND TRACIE RUIZ

CAREER RESULTS IN MAJOR COMPETITIONS

Year	Competition	Finish in Duet
1984	Olympic Games	First
	Nationals/Olympic Trials	First
1983	Pan American Games	First
	American Cup II	First
	U.S. Championships	First
	National Sports Festival	First
1982	World Swimming Championships	Second
	U.S. Championships	First
	Moscow Invitational	First
	Association of Intercollegiate Athletics for Women	First
1981	Pan Pacific Championships	First
	U.S. Championships	First
	National Sports Festival	First

1984 OLYMPIC GAMES

Figures

1. Ruiz 99.467
5. Costie 93.700

Average 96.584

Routine Finals

1. U.S.A. (Costie & Ruiz) 99.000

Final Standings

Medal	Team	Figures	Routine	Total
Gold	U.S.A. (Costie & Ruiz)	96.584	99.000	195.584
Silver	Canada (Hambrook & Kryczka)	96.034	98.200	194.234
Bronze	Japan (Simura & Motoyoshi)	90.992	97.000	187.992

INDEX